THE
HOME
BARTENDER

WHISKEY

CIDER MILL PRESS

BOOK
PUBLISHERS

140+ ESSENTIAL COCKTAILS
for the **WHISKEY LOVER**

THE HOME BARTENDER: WHISKEY

13-Digit ISBN: 978-1-40034-611-0
10-Digit ISBN: 1-40034-611-8

This book may be ordered by mail from the publisher. Please include $5.99 for postage and handling. Please support your local bookseller first!

Books published by Cider Mill Press Book Publishers are available at special discounts for bulk purchases in the United States by corporations, institutions, and other organizations. For more information, please contact the publisher.

Cider Mill Press Book Publishers

"Where good books are ready for press"

501 Nelson Place
Nashville, Tennessee 37214
cidermillpress.com

Image Credits: Photos on pages 17, 26, 30, 38, 41, 42, 49, 64, 72, 79, 88, 101, 105, 114, 121, 133, 134, 138, 155, 160, 164, 176, 180, 183, 187, 188, 191, 192, 200, 209, 210, 225, 230, 264, 295, 296, and 299 used under official license from Shutterstock.com.

All other images courtesy of Cider Mill Press Book Publishers.

Glassware icons by Shutterstock; all ingredient icons by Shutterstock or Cider Mill Press Book Publishers.

Printed in Canada

24 25 26 27 28 FR 5 4 3 2 1
First Edition

CONTENTS

SOPHISTICATED SIPPERS 149

SOUR SATISFACTION 207

EXTRA EASY AND SUPER SIMPLE 241

INDEX 300

INTRODUCTION

Cocktails can be complicated. With so many drinks featuring what feels like dozens of ingredients, being mixed together in increasingly complicated and diverse ways, it isn't hard to feel out of your depth when it comes to mixology.

But it doesn't have to be that way! Some of the best cocktails in the world feature only a couple of ingredients, shaken or stirred together in straightforward proportions, and ready to drink in seconds. Everyone knows that sometimes simplicity is the way to go—not just for the sake of convenience, but for taste as well. After all, who needs eight different ingredients muddling their flavors together, when all you really want is something to accent the great taste of your whiskey?

The Home Bartender series features the best of the best when it comes to simple cocktails. With classic cocktails you'll recognize and new drinks you're sure to love, there's something for everyone here. Whether you're looking for some novel and unique drinks or to bust out an old and timeless recipe, *The Home Bartender: Whiskey* is the perfect book for any home bar!

BAR TOOLS

Sometimes mixing a drink is as simple as pouring the ingredients. Other times, you need to do a little more. Bar tools are there to make your life a bit easier when it comes to mixing up these more complicated cocktails. From the cocktail shaker to the muddler, these are the tools that you would be wise to have in your home bar.

Must-Haves	Nice to Have
Cocktail Shaker	Cocktail Stirrer
Strainer	Muddler
Jigger	Juicer
Knife	Zester
Bottle Opener	
Corkscrew	

GLASSWARE

Must-Haves	Nice to Have	Wish List
Pint Glass	Margarita Glass	Hurricane Glass
Shot Glass	Cocktail Glass	Daiquiri Glass
Rocks Glass	Champagne Flute	Irish Coffee Glass
Highball Glass	Mason Jar	Sour Glass

Though every type and label of whiskey has its own distinct and nuanced flavor profile, it can generally be said that whiskey is a bold and complex spirit. It has a presence all its own and shouldn't be thrown carelessly into just any mixed drink. This is not to say that whiskey can't be versatile but that any good whiskey cocktail should be thoughtfully built with ingredients that balance and complement the whiskey. Within these pages, you'll find all manner of cocktails, whether you're looking for something tart and refreshing or something darker with a little more moxie.

Of course, there are certainly those who maintain that whiskey is best served neat or on the rocks. Yet whiskey cocktails have been around since the cocktail's invention and rank among the most iconic of old-school drinks— the aptly named Old Fashioned, the Manhattan, the Sazerac, the Mint Julep, and the Boulevardier, to name a few. The origins of these legendary drinks are almost as storied as the history of whiskey itself. The earliest incarnations of the cocktail date back to the early 1800s and for the most part were relatively straightforward combinations of alcohol, bitters, sugar, and water. Many of the whiskey cocktails that have since become tried-and-true classics follow that exact formula. What's more, the recent revival of interest in classic cocktail culture has seen all kinds of innovative bitters, shrubs, and syrups come on the scene.

In this book, we've got everything from the quintessential whiskey cocktails to adventurous new creations. Many of them have been crafted either by or for the very distilleries behind our favorite whiskeys, including Jack Daniel's, Corsair, Hartfield & Co., Maker's Mark, Jim Beam, Willett, and Buffalo Trace, ensuring that they are expertly tailored to suit the label used in the recipe.

While we've recommended specific brands or labels in some recipes, you can always test out alternatives. Do some research to find whiskeys with comparable flavor profiles or experiment and try something totally different. The joy of crafting cocktails at home is that you get to make them exactly how you like them.

SIMPLE SYRUP

Place 1 cup sugar and 1 cup water in a saucepan and bring it to a boil, stirring to dissolve the sugar. Remove the pan from heat and let the syrup cool completely before using or storing.

THE CLASSICS

Whiskey is a star all by itself, but sometimes a star shines even more brightly in the presence of supporting elements. This chapter includes those most classic combinations, where whiskey is perfectly matched with ingredients that bring out and elevate its flavor. From standards as simple as the Jack & Cola to truly iconic drinks like the Old Fashioned to more complex favorites like the Vieux Carré, all the most beloved and well-known whiskey cocktails can be found here.

JACK & COLA

An all-time classic, this iconic pairing of flavors has inspired a slew of culinary inventions, from barbecue sauces to Popsicles.

INGREDIENTS

1 oz. Jack Daniel's Old No. 7 Tennessee Whiskey

3 oz. cola

1 lime slice (garnish)

GLASSWARE

Collins glass

1 Fill a glass with ice and build the drink in it, adding the ingredients (except the garnish) in the order they are listed.

2 Gently stir until chilled and garnish with the lime slice.

WHISKEY SLING

This drink takes its inspiration from the Singapore Sling, a gin cocktail developed at the Raffles Hotel in Singapore near the turn of the century.

INGREDIENTS

 2 oz. Tennessee whiskey

 ½ oz. lemon juice

 ¾ oz. simple syrup (see page 7)

 2 dashes orange bitters

 1 lemon slice (garnish)

GLASSWARE
 Rocks glass

1 Place all of the ingredients, except for the garnish, in a cocktail shaker, fill it two-thirds of the way with ice, and shake until chilled.

2 Strain over ice into a glass, garnish with the lemon slice, and enjoy.

SINGLE BARREL OLD FASHIONED

Jack Daniel's robust Single Barrel Select Tennessee Whiskey elevates this classic cocktail (courtesy of Jack Daniel's).

INGREDIENTS

 I orange slice

 2 oz. Jack Daniel's Single Barrel Select Tennessee whiskey

 3/4 oz. simple syrup (see page 7)

 2 dashes bitters

 I maraschino cherry (garnish)

 orange peel (garnish)

GLASSWARE

 Rocks glass

1 Muddle the orange slice in the bottom of a rocks glass.

2 Fill the glass with ice and build the drink in it, adding the ingredients (except the garnish) in the order they are listed.

3 Gently stir until chilled and garnish with the cherry and orange peel.

CLASSIC OLD FASHIONED

It's hard to anoint a "favorite" whiskey cocktail, but the Old Fashioned certainly challenges for the spot. Featuring simple syrup, bitters, and a little bit of citrus to accent the flavor of the whiskey, the Old Fashioned is a sophisticated drink for the seasoned whiskey drinker. For the classic version of the cocktail, an underrated, extremely drinkable whiskey like Maker's Mark is perfect.

INGREDIENTS

 1 splash simple syrup (see page 7)

 1 orange peel strip

 2 drops bitters

 2 oz. Maker's Mark bourbon whiskey

 Club soda (optional)

 Lemon peel (garnish)

GLASSWARE

 Rocks glass

1. Add the simple syrup to a rocks glass and drop in a strip of orange peel. Add the bitters and muddle together.

2. Fill the glass with ice, then add your bourbon. Stir together slowly. Add club soda if desired.

3. Garnish with a lemon peel.

PERFECT OLD FASHIONED

For the Perfect Old Fashioned, eschew the simple syrup in favor of a sugar cube and some water, and rely on the orange wedge garnish for the small punch of citrus the drink requires. Using a top-shelf whiskey like Woodford Reserve will enhance the drinkability of the cocktail while still keeping you in a reasonable price range. Sure, you could spend hundreds of dollars on bourbon. But if you do that, you probably aren't watering it down in a cocktail, no matter how delicious it may be.

INGREDIENTS

 I sugar cube

 2 drops bitters

 I splash water

 2 oz. Woodford Reserve bourbon whiskey

 I orange wedge (garnish)

 I maraschino cherry (garnish)

GLASSWARE
 Rocks glass

1 Add the sugar cube to your glass. Add 2 drops bitters. Add a small splash of water and muddle.

2 Fill the glass with ice and add the bourbon. Stir lightly. Garnish with an orange wedge and a maraschino cherry.

OLD FASHIONED EGGNOG

This recipe yields 5 pints of the grandest eggnog ever ladled into a cup. An original Four Roses creation, this recipe dates all the way back to 1936!

INGREDIENTS

 6 eggs, separated

 3/4 cup sugar

 1 pint cream

 1 pint milk

 1 pint bourbon

 1 oz. Jamaican rum

 Grated nutmeg (garnish)

GLASSWARE

 Rocks glass

1 Beat the yolks and whites of six eggs separately.

2 Add ½ cup of sugar to the yolks while beating.

3 Add ¼ cup of sugar to whites after beating until very stiff.

4 Mix egg whites with yolks, and stir in one pint of cream and one pint of milk.

5 Add a pint of bourbon and 1 oz. of rum, and stir thoroughly.

6 Serve cold with grated nutmeg.

FOUR ROSES COLLINS

The original gin-based Tom Collins rocketed to fame in the late nineteenth century—so much so that it inspired the name of the Collins glass. This 1959 incarnation from Four Roses isn't quite as old but cements the Collins cocktail as one of the greats.

INGREDIENTS

 1½ oz. Four Roses bourbon

 Juice of 1 lemon

 1 teaspoon sugar

 Club soda

 1 lemon rind (garnish)

 Maraschino cherries (garnish)

GLASSWARE
 Highball glass

1 Pour a jigger of Four Roses into a tall glass over cubed ice.

2 Add the juice of one lemon, followed by sugar, to the drink. Fill with club soda and stir.

3 Garnish with lemon rind and cherries and serve.

JACK DANIEL'S BOULEVARDIER

The bittersweet Boulevardier dates back to the 1920s and first appeared in print in 1927, in the Harry's New York Bar in Paris manual, *Barflies and Cocktails*. Its invention is attributed to American writer and socialite Erskine Gwynne, who ran the literary magazine *Boulevardier*. We recommend using Jack Daniel's Single Barrel Proof.

INGREDIENTS

 1½ oz. whiskey

 ½ oz. dry vermouth

 ½ oz. Campari

 1 orange peel (garnish)

GLASSWARE

 Coupe

1   Place all of the ingredients, except for the garnish, in a cocktail shaker, fill it two-thirds of the way with ice, and shake until chilled.

2   Strain over ice into a glass, garnish with the orange peel, and enjoy.

CLASSIC MANHATTAN

Whiskey and vermouth are a classic combination that's difficult to go wrong with. The Manhattan makes use of this simple combination and, with the addition of just a few drops of bitters, creates something truly fantastic. A refined and elegant cocktail, the Classic Manhattan offers the everyday mixologist a simple way to enjoy an old classic.

INGREDIENTS

 2 oz. Knob Creek rye whiskey

 2/3 oz. sweet vermouth

 2 drops bitters

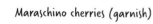 Maraschino cherries (garnish)

GLASSWARE
 Cocktail glass

1 Fill a mixing glass with ice and add the liquid ingredients. Stir gently to avoid bruising the drink.

2 Strain the resulting mixture into a cocktail glass.

3 Garnish with a cherry or two.

PERFECT MANHATTAN

When it comes to a cocktail as classy as the Manhattan, why settle for anything less than the finest ingredients? By building your drink around top-shelf whiskey, you can be sure that you're getting the best tasting Manhattan around. The Perfect Manhattan is made using WhistlePig Straight Rye, one of the most delicious whiskeys the average person can get their hands on.

INGREDIENTS

 2 oz. Whistlepig Straight Rye whiskey

 ⅔ oz. sweet vermouth

 2 drops bitters

 1 maraschino cherry (garnish)

GLASSWARE

 Coupe

1 Fill a mixing glass with ice and add the liquid ingredients. Stir gently to avoid bruising the drink.

2 Put a maraschino cherry in the bottom of a cocktail glass and strain the contents of the mixing glass over it.

BUDGET MANHATTAN

One of the great things about the Manhattan is its adaptability. While tradition dictates that it be made with rye whiskey, contemporary mixologists have begun to use bourbon with increasing regularity. And chances are, you're more likely to have some affordable bourbon lying around than you are rye whiskey. So why not make a Budget Manhattan? It might not be by the book (although if you're following these instructions, it technically is now), but it still packs a punch, as well as a rich, delicious flavor.

INGREDIENTS

2 oz. Jim Beam bourbon

2/3 oz. sweet vermouth

2 drops bitters

1 maraschino cherry (garnish)

GLASSWARE

Rocks glass

1 Fill a mixing glass with ice and add the bourbon, vermouth, and bitters. Stir gently to avoid bruising the drink.

2 Strain the mixture over ice into a rocks glass. Garnish with a cherry.

ROB ROY

The Rob Roy is essentially a Manhattan for those who prefer Scotch. Made with simply whiskey, vermouth, and bitters, the Rob Roy swaps out rye whiskey (or bourbon) in favor of Scotch's smoky flavor. The Rob Roy hasn't attained quite the same level of popularity as its rye-based contemporary, but it is no less delicious. As with many cocktails, your stance on the matter comes down to personal preference.

INGREDIENTS

2 oz. Scotch whisky

1 oz. sweet vermouth

2 drops bitters

1 maraschino cherry (garnish)

GLASSWARE

Cocktail glass

1 Fill a mixing glass with ice and add the liquid ingredients. Stir gently to avoid bruising the drink.

2 Add a maraschino cherry to your cocktail glass and strain the contents of the mixing glass over it.

HOT TODDY

Whiskey is the perfect liquor choice for autumn or winter because it lends itself so well to warm drinks. While you could simply spike a mug of warm apple cider or add a dose to your hot chocolate, the Hot Toddy is a classic cocktail passed down through the ages. With a more well-rounded flavor than those simple suggestions, this classic is sure to warm you up quickly after a long day of snowshoeing. Customize this winter favorite with a little added mint flavor!

INGREDIENTS

 1 oz. honey

 2 mint leaves

 4 oz. tea

 2 oz. whiskey

 Lemon juice (to taste)

GLASSWARE

 Glass mug

1 Add the honey to your mug or heat-proof glass. Allow it time to spread across the bottom of the mug, and then muddle the mint leaves into it.

2 Boil some water and make a serving of your favorite tea. Set aside.

3 Add the whiskey and lemon juice to your drink. Use as much lemon as you might typically take with your tea.

4 Top the drink off with the tea you set aside earlier. Stir the mixture together lightly and enjoy.

VIEUX CARRÉ

One of the Big Easy's many contributions to cocktail history, the Vieux Carré was created by head bartender Walter Bergeron at the Hotel Monteleone in 1938. This complex sipping cocktail, which uses two types of bitters, evokes the languorous decadence of New Orleans. We recommend using Jack Daniel's Tennessee Rye.

INGREDIENTS

 ³/₄ oz. rye whiskey

 ³/₄ oz. cognac

 ³/₄ oz. Noilly Prat Rouge sweet vermouth

 ¹/₄ teaspoon Bénédictine liqueur

 2 dashes Peychaud's bitters

 2 dashes Angostura bitters

 1 lemon twist (garnish)

GLASSWARE

 Rocks glass

1 Combine ingredients, except for the garnish, in a rocks glass, add ice, and stir. Add garnish and serve.

CLASSIC MINT JULEP

Who doesn't love a mint julep? The classic drink of the Kentucky Derby, the mint julep has remained popular with whiskey drinkers for more than a hundred years. With a mid-range drinkable bourbon and a little powdered sugar (the powdered sugar is important if you want to do it right), this cocktail is sure to see many new converts after just one taste.

INGREDIENTS

 4 mint leaves

 1 teaspoon powdered sugar

 1 splash water

 2 oz. Maker's Mark bourbon whiskey

 1 mint sprig (garnish)

GLASSWARE
 Rocks glass

1 Tear the mint leaves in half to release their flavor, then muddle in the bottom of your glass with powdered sugar and water.

2 Fill the glass with cracked ice, then add the bourbon. Stir gently.

3 Garnish with a sprig of mint.

PERFECT MINT JULEP

Why not take the mint julep to a bit more high-end place? If you truly appreciate subtle flavor and nuance (and are willing to spend a bit extra on the best bourbon), you can make your mint julep a truly transcendent drinking experience. Be sure you drink it out of a silver or pewter cup. If you're going to call something "perfect," you'd better go all the way. The Perfect Mint Julep does just that.

INGREDIENTS

 4 mint leaves

 1 teaspoon powdered sugar

 1 splash water

 2 oz. Woodford Reserve bourbon whiskey

 1 mint sprig (garnish)

GLASSWARE

 Silver or pewter cup

1 Muddle the mint leaves in the bottom of the cup with powdered sugar and water.

2 Fill the cup with cracked ice, then add your bourbon. Stir until the outside of your cup is visibly chilled.

3 Garnish with a sprig of mint.

BUDGET MINT JULEP

So you want a mint julep, but you don't have the ingredients to do it exactly as described? No matter. There is a way to make a perfectly acceptable mint julep with whatever you have on hand. The beauty of the mint julep is that while it has a reputation for being a refined cocktail, the ingredients are simple enough that just about anyone can make it (as long as you've got some mint on hand!).

INGREDIENTS

 4 mint leaves

 1 teaspoon sugar

 1 splash water

 2 oz. Evan Williams bourbon whiskey

 1 mint sprig (garnish)

GLASSWARE
Rocks glass

1 Never mind the powdered sugar; regular sugar will work just fine. Muddle the sugar in your glass with the water and mint leaves (tear them in half to release additional flavor).

2 Fill the glass with ice, then add your bourbon. Stir gently.

3 Garnish with a sprig of mint.

BELLINI

The Bellini was originally created by Giuseppe Cipriani, founder of the famed Harry's Bar in Venice, Italy. Frequented by stars and luminaries such as Ernest Hemingway, Truman Capote, and Aristotle Onassis, Harry's Bar was the epitome of café society glamour, which this drink certainly evokes. We recommend adding a kick with Jack Daniel's Gentleman Jack.

INGREDIENTS

1 oz. Tennessee whiskey

1 oz. peach puree

Champagne

GLASSWARE

Coupe

1 Combine whiskey and peach purée in a glass.

2 Top off the drink with champagne.

SAZERAC

The official cocktail of New Orleans—the Sazerac—originated in Antoine Peychaud's apothecary on Rue Royal in the 1830s. Since then, it has evolved into the harmonious blend of bitters, anise, and rye that we know today. We recommend using Jack Daniel's Single Barrel Rye.

INGREDIENTS

1½ oz. rye whiskey

2 dashes Peychaud's bitters

1 dash Angostura bitters

1 bar spoon absinthe

1 lemon peel (garnish)

GLASSWARE
Rocks glass

1   Fill a glass with ice and build the drink in it, adding the ingredients (except the garnish) in the order they are listed.

2   Gently stir until chilled and garnish with the lemon peel.

IRISH COFFEE

The perfect wake-up cocktail and a favorite drink of airport bar patrons (or maybe that's just me). Irish Coffee is made a variety of different ways—with some including Irish Cream, some not, some specifying Irish whiskey, some not. But it just doesn't feel like "Irish" Coffee without Jameson and Bailey's, does it?

INGREDIENTS

3 oz. coffee

1 dash sugar

1 oz. Irish whiskey

1 oz. Bailey's Irish Cream liqueur

Whipped cream (garnish)

GLASSWARE

Irish coffee glass or a mug

1 Pour the coffee into your glass or mug and add the sugar to it. Stir until the sugar has dissolved.

2 Add the whiskey and stir again.

3 Top the drink with Irish cream. If you can, layer the cream on top rather than stirring it in.

4 Garnish with a dollop of whipped cream and enjoy!

BROWN DERBY

Let's take things to a classy place with the Brown Derby, a classic whiskey cocktail that doesn't try too hard to overwhelm you with complex flavors. Made with grapefruit juice, whiskey, and honey, this simple and refreshing cocktail proves that when it comes to ingredients, less is often more. The Brown Derby allows the sweet grapefruit juice to play off the whiskey, dulling the sharp edge of the grapefruit flavor only slightly with the addition of a spoonful of honey.

INGREDIENTS

 2 oz. maple whiskey

 2 oz. grapefruit juice

 ½ oz. honey

 1 grapefruit slice, quartered (garnish)

GLASSWARE

 Mason jar

1. Fill a cocktail shaker with ice and add the maple whiskey, grapefruit juice, and honey. Shake vigorously until thoroughly mixed.

2. Add ice to your glass and strain the cocktail shaker into it.

3. Garnish with a slice of grapefruit and enjoy!

FLASHY FUN

Whiskey can be served simply, but who says it can't get a little more exciting? This chapter is full of drinks with new and exciting flavor combinations, along with some unique ingredients and garnishes to make things even more thrilling. With beautiful displays like those found in the Modern Toddy, A Dark Art, the Seahorse, and cocktails you'd never have thought of, such as the Derby Season or the Bourbon Ice Cream, you're sure to find something to tickle your fancy.

WHISKEY NUT

If you're from the South, chances are you've dropped a handful of peanuts into your cola before. Why this is only Southern tradition is a mystery; people everywhere are well aware of the delicious combo that is sugar and salt. The Whiskey Nut takes the sweet and salty partnership and adds a dose of whiskey and orange to give you something new and impressive to show off.

INGREDIENTS

 2 oz. whiskey

 1 dash orange liqueur

 2 drops peanut extract

 6 oz. cola

 1 orange slice (garnish)

 1 handful peanuts (garnish)

GLASSWARE
 Rocks glass

1 Fill a rocks glass halfway with ice and then add the whiskey and orange liqueur (just enough to taste).

2 Add a small dash of peanut extract and fill the glass with cola.

3 Garnish the mixture with an orange slice and a handful of peanuts. You can either eat them on the side or pop them right into the glass like you would with a can of cola!

TWISTED JULEP

Extra-aged Jim Beam Black, peach nectar, and brown sugar add a little more moxie to this twist on the mint julep.

INGREDIENTS

 4 mint leaves

 A touch of brown sugar

 Blueberries

 2 oz. Jim Beam Black bourbon

 ½ oz. peach nectar

 Blueberries (garnish)

 1 mint sprig (garnish)

GLASSWARE
 Tin

1 In a tin or double rocks glass, muddle the mint and brown sugar. Add the blueberries and muddle again.

2 Add crushed ice and Jim Beam Black. Stir to distribute mint.

3 Top with crushed ice. Garnish with leftover blueberries and a mint sprig.

CUBISM

Now here's a unique cocktail—one that is as much about presentation as it is about taste. Bourbon, Cognac, rum, and Fernet Branca Menta might not seem like they go together at first glance, but like a Picasso painting, there is far more to this cocktail than meets the eye. The inclusion of cherry gelatin along the rim of the glass might seem unnecessary at first, but it adds to the whimsical feel of a cocktail that is as fun to look at as it is to drink.

INGREDIENTS

 1 oz. Bulleit Bourbon

 2 teaspoons Cognac

 2 teaspoons Diplomático Reserva Exclusiva Rum

 2 teaspoons simple syrup (see page 7)

 1 teaspoon Fernet Branca Menta

 1 strip lemon zest

 4 drops cherry gelatin (garnish)

GLASSWARE

 Rocks glass

1 Place all of the ingredients (except the cherry gelatin) in a mixing glass, fill it two-thirds of the way with ice, and stir until chilled.

2 Strain over a large ice cube into the rocks glass, apply the four drops of cherry gelatin just below the rim of the glass, making sure they are parallel to the rim, and enjoy.

TEMPTATION

Floral and citrus flavors combine with a hint of that signature rye spice to make this tempting, spirit-forward cocktail.

INGREDIENTS

1 1/2 oz. rye whiskey

1/2 oz. Dubonnet Blonde

1/2 oz. triple sec

1/2 oz. Pernod

GLASSWARE

Rocks glass or highball glass

1 Place all of the ingredients in a cocktail shaker, fill it two-thirds of the way with ice, and shake until chilled.

2 Strain into a glass and enjoy.

UTOPIA

California's St. George Spirits has become one of the very best craft producers in the world, expertly fashioning everything from whiskey, gin, and brandy to shochu and bitters. Their Spiced Pear Liqueur is a must for your home bar, supplying the warming and delicate flavors present in a well-made pastry.

INGREDIENTS

 1½ oz. Redemption rye whiskey

 ½ oz. St. George Spiced Pear Liqueur

 ½ oz. vanilla simple syrup (see recipe to the right)

 2 dashes Fee Brothers black walnut bitters

 1 dehydrated apple slice (garnish)

GLASSWARE

 Rocks glass

1 Place all of the ingredients , except for the garnish, in a mixing glass, fill it two-thirds of the way with ice, and stir until chilled.

2 Strain the cocktail over a large ice cube into the rocks glass, garnish with the dehydrated apple slice, and enjoy.

VANILLA SIMPLE SYRUP

Place 1 cup water in a small saucepan and bring it to a boil. Add 2 cups sugar and stir until it has dissolved. Remove the pan from heat. Halve 1 vanilla bean and scrape the seeds into the syrup. Cut the vanilla bean pod into thirds and add the pieces to the syrup. Stir to combine, cover the pan, and let the mixture sit at room temperature for 12 hours. Strain the syrup through cheesecloth before using or storing.

THE THIRD MAN

Finding a single malt where one would expect a gin is far from the only surprise in this cocktail.

INGREDIENTS

 2 oz. single malt Scotch whisky

 ¾ oz. St-Germain

 ¾ oz. lemon juice

 1 egg white

 GLASSWARE
Rocks glass

1 Place all of the ingredients in a cocktail shaker, fill it two-thirds of the way with ice, and shake until chilled.

2 Strain into a rocks glass.

BLACKBERRY SAGE JULEP

Sage and blackberry make such a great combination, especially in a julep. One really enhances the flavor of the other. We recommend using Elijah Craig bourbon.

INGREDIENTS

 2 blackberries

 1 sage sprig

 1/2 oz. turbinado or Demerara simple syrup

 2 oz. bourbon

 Crushed ice

 1 blackberry (garnish)

 1 sage sprig (garnish)

GLASSWARE
 Highball glass

1 Lightly muddle two blackberries in a shaker tin and add one sage sprig. Add remaining ingredients and shake lightly, for just long enough to mix the ingredients together.

2 Fine strain into a glass or julep tin, and cover with crushed ice to create a small snow cone over the top of the tin.

3 Garnish with sage sprig and blackberry. Serve with straws.

HEARTS ON FIRE

At once earthy, fruity, and spicy, this bold cocktail definitely leaves an impression.

INGREDIENTS

 2 oz. bourbon

 ¾ oz. Chambord

 ½ oz. maraschino liqueur

 2 dashes Hellfire bitters

 2 brandy-soaked cherries (garnish)

GLASSWARE

 Rocks glass

1 Pour ingredients, except for the garnish, into cocktail glass and stir. Garnish with two brandy-soaked cherries.

NIGHT FEVER

Between the rye and Domaine de Canton, this cocktail's got quite a kick.

INGREDIENTS

 1¼ oz. rye whiskey

 ¾ oz. sweet vermouth

 ½ oz. Domaine de Canton

 1 dash of Angostura bitters

 1 strip lemon peel (garnish)

GLASSWARE

 Rocks glass

1   Chill a rocks glass in the freezer.

2   Add the rye, vermouth, Domaine de Canton, and bitters to a mixing glass, fill it two-thirds of the way with ice, and stir until chilled.

3   Strain into the chilled glass over ice and garnish with the strip of lemon peel.

MODERN TODDY

This modern take on a classic Hot Toddy takes the basic foundation of lemon, honey, and whiskey, and incorporates a series of garnishes designed to impart an extra hint of flavor. Make this cozy cocktail to your taste by adjusting the amount of lemon and honey used. The apple, star anise, cinnamon, and rosemary elevate the drink with a subtly spiced, herbaceous quality.

INGREDIENTS

 4 oz. hot water

 1 oz. whiskey

 Honey, to taste

 Lemon juice, to taste

 1 rosemary sprig (garnish)

 1 apple slice (garnish)

 1 lemon slice (garnish)

 1 cinnamon stick (garnish)

 1 star anise pod (garnish)

GLASSWARE

 Mug

1 Boil the water as you would for tea.

2 Add the whiskey to a mug, then top with the boiled water.

3 Add honey and lemon juice as desired.

4 Garnish with an apple slice, rosemary sprig, lemon slice, cinnamon stick, and star anise pod.

IRISH ROSE

With its rosy color, the Irish Rose is an attractive alternative to the more common whiskey cocktails. The unusual combination of whiskey and lemon-lime soda works surprisingly well, especially with the subtle flavor of grenadine bridging the gap.

INGREDIENTS

 2 oz. Irish whiskey

 3 oz. lemon-lime soda

 1 oz. grenadine

 1 lime wedge (garnish)

GLASSWARE
Rocks glass

1 Add ice to your glass, then add in the whiskey and lemon-lime soda.

2 Top with a splash of grenadine and stir together until a rosy color is achieved.

3 Garnish with a wedge of lime.

BLACK SESAME ORGEAT

INGREDIENTS

½ cup black sesame seeds

2 cups hot water

3 cups sugar

½ teaspoon orange flower water

2 tablespoons vodka

1 Toast sesame seeds for 1–2 minutes over medium heat. Set aside to cool.

2 In a bowl, stir together hot water and sugar until dissolved.

3 Combine the syrup and sesame seeds in a blender or food processor and blend for 1–2 minutes. Set aside and leave to steep for 3–12 hours.

4 Strain the mixture through 2–3 layers of cheesecloth, squeezing as you go. Discard ground sesame seeds or set aside for later use.

5 Add orange flower water and vodka. Bottle the syrup, which will keep for about two weeks.

A DARK ART

Sophisticated, striking, and sure to impress anyone you make it for, A Dark Art pairs Maker's 46 with the nutty caramel flavor of black sesame orgeat.

INGREDIENTS

 1½ oz. Maker's Mark 46 bourbon whisky

 ½ oz. black sesame orgeat (see recipe on opposite page)

 1 lime

 13 dashes Angostura bitters

 1 pinch activated charcoal (garnish)

 Jasmine flower (garnish)

GLASSWARE

 Coupe

1   Place all of the ingredients, except for the garnish, in a cocktail shaker, fill it two-thirds of the way with ice, and shake until chilled.

2   Strain into a coupe, garnish with the activated charcoal and jasmine flower, and enjoy.

SINGED SAZERAC

It would be much, much too easy to list the Old Fashioned here. But the truth is, the Old Fashioned doesn't really feel, well, old fashioned. It's a timeless cocktail, as popular now as it was a hundred years ago. The Sazerac, on the other hand, is less well known but is widely regarded as the world's oldest cocktail. This take on a classic Sazerac eschews the usual Peychaud's bitters in favor of orange bitters, paired with a burnt orange rind garnish.

INGREDIENTS

 ⅓ oz. absinthe

 2 oz. rye whiskey

 1 sugar cube or 1 splash simple syrup (see page 7)

 2 dashes orange bitters

 1 orange rind (garnish)

GLASSWARE

 Rocks glass

1. Rinse the rocks glass with absinthe. Discard any excess absinthe pooled at the bottom of the glass and fill with ice.

2. Add the whiskey, sugar cube, and orange bitters to a cocktail shaker filled with ice. Shake well.

3. Strain the resulting mixture into the rocks glass.

4. Using a brulee torch, lightly singe a strip of orange rind to bring out its bitter citrus flavor. Add to the glass as garnish.

DERBY SEASON

Rosé and bourbon might seem like somewhat of an odd coupling, but as with any good cocktail, it's all about getting the proportions right. Try it! We promise you won't regret it.

INGREDIENTS

 2 oz. Jim Beam Black bourbon

 ¾ oz. lemon juice

 ¾ oz. simple syrup (see page 7)

 ½ oz. dry rosé

 1 lemon peel (garnish)

 GLASSWARE
Wine glass

1 Stir the Jim Beam, lemon juice, and simple syrup in a mixing glass.

2 Pour the drink over ice and top with the rosé.

3 Garnish with a lemon peel and serve.

SEAHORSE

The name of this large batch cocktail is inspired by Old Bardstown Bottled in Bond Bourbon, which was named for a famous racehorse of the same name from Calumet Farm in Lexington, Kentucky.

INGREDIENTS

 750 milliliter bottle of Old Bardstown Bottled in Bond, Kentucky straight bourbon whiskey

 1 gallon orange juice

 1 full cap blood orange bitters (Stirrings brand recommended)

 4 oz. simple syrup (see page 7)

 1 thick slice star fruit pre-soaked in bourbon (garnish)

 Luxardo syrup (garnish)

GLASSWARE

 Wine glass

1 Combine ingredients, except for the garnishes, in a large punch bowl. Chill in the refrigerator. Garnish each drink with a slice of star fruit and a drizzle of Luxardo syrup.

JACK JULEP

Jack Daniel's riff on the traditional mint julep swaps out bourbon for charcoal-mellowed Tennessee whiskey.

INGREDIENTS

 2 oz. Jack Daniel's Tennessee whiskey

 1 dash sugar

 1 mint sprig (garnish)

GLASSWARE:

 Rocks glass

1 Place all of the ingredients, except for the garnish, in a cocktail shaker, fill it two-thirds of the way with ice, and shake until chilled.

2 Strain over ice into a rocks glass, garnish with the sprig of mint, and enjoy.

TENNESSEE MULE

If you prefer a spicier ginger beer to ginger ale, this is your drink. At once warming and refreshing, the Tennessee Mule is a cocktail for all seasons. We recommend using Jack Daniel's Old No. 7.

INGREDIENTS

 1 oz. Tennessee whiskey

 1 squeeze fresh lime juice

 3 parts ginger beer

 1 lime slice (garnish)

 1 mint (garnish)

GLASSWARE
 Copper mug

1 Fill a glass with ice and build the drink in it, adding the ingredients, except for the garnish, in the order they are listed.

2 Gently stir until chilled and garnish with the lime slice and mint.

BOURBON ICE CREAM

Some people shy away from using milk or cream in cocktails, and that's understandable. Milk has such a distinctive flavor that it's difficult to imagine it mixing well with the inherent bite of alcohol. That said, if you enjoy a White Russian, you'll want to give Bourbon Ice Cream a try. A little milk, a little vanilla, and a little sugar give this drink a delicious "melted milkshake" quality.

INGREDIENTS

1 oz. bourbon whiskey

2 oz. whole milk

1 dash simple syrup (see page 7)

2 to 3 drops vanilla extract

1 dash nutmeg (garnish)

1 cinnamon stick (garnish)

GLASSWARE
Rocks glass

1 Place all of the ingredients, except for the garnish, in a cocktail shaker, fill it two-thirds of the way with ice, and shake until chilled.

2 Strain into a glass, garnish with the dash of nutmeg and a cinnamon stick, and enjoy.

SPITFIRE

Take the name as a warning—this bold, sweet cocktail has a real kick!

INGREDIENTS

 I oz. whiskey

 I oz. dark rum

 I oz. cherry vodka

GLASSWARE

Shot glass

1   Place all of the ingredients in a cocktail shaker, fill it two-thirds of the way with ice, and shake until chilled.

2   Strain into a glass and enjoy.

BOURBON BALL MILKSHAKE

This seriously rich and indulgent spiked milkshake marries smooth bourbon cream with ice cream, fudge, and candied pecans. Decadence in a glass.

INGREDIENTS

 4 scoops vanilla bean ice cream

 2 oz. Buffalo Trace Bourbon Cream

 2 oz. chocolate fudge

 Chocolate syrup

 Whipped cream

 Candied pecans (garnish)

GLASSWARE

 Tin mug or rocks glass

1 Combine ice cream, bourbon cream liquor, and chocolate fudge in a blender. Decorate the inside of a frozen glass with drizzles of chocolate syrup.

2 Pour milkshake into glass and top with whipped cream, more chocolate syrup, and candied pecans, if desired.

DEAL BREAKER

A touch of absinthe gives this cocktail an inventive and unexpected twist.

INGREDIENTS

 2 oz. Corsair Quinoa whiskey

 ½ oz. honey

 2 dashes Peychaud's bitters

 Absinthe

 1 dash rhubarb bitters

 Orange slice, halved (garnish)

GLASSWARE
 Rocks glass

1   Stir and strain the whiskey, the honey, and the Peychaud's bitters into a rocks glass rinsed with absinthe and rhubarb bitters.

2   Don't add ice, and garnish with an orange slice.

POMEGRANATE SMASH

Though pomegranate and bourbon may seem like an unexpected combination, these two really make a great pairing. We recommend using Maker's Mark 46.

INGREDIENTS

 2 oz. bourbon

 1 oz. POM Wonderful pomegranate juice

 ½ oz. honey

 ½ oz. lemon juice

 Pomegranate seeds (garnish)

GLASSWARE

 Rocks glass

1 Place all of the ingredients, except for the garnish, in a cocktail shaker, fill it two-thirds of the way with ice, and shake until chilled.

2 Strain over ice into a rocks glass, garnish with the pomegranate seeds, and enjoy.

SHARING IS CARING

The only thing better than a good whiskey cocktail is a batch that you can share with your friends. Here you'll find a wealth of drinks that can be made to share with flavor profiles that are sure to please even your pickiest pals. With cocktails for every occasion—from the Renegade Lemonade for your spring fling to the Spiced Punch perfect for a holiday party—your guests will never go thirsty. That being said, no one would judge if you wanted to make one of these and it keep it all to yourself—we won't tell!

WHISKEY PUNCH

Plenty of people make punches with vodka, gin, or even rum, but few are bold enough to make a punch with whiskey as the base ingredient. This whiskey punch recipe is a surprisingly tasty take on the idea, with orange juice and tea standing up to the flavor of the whiskey in a big way. The end result is a whiskey drink cut with citrusy freshness—a memorable harmony of flavors.

INGREDIENTS

 2 oz. whiskey

 2 oz. iced tea

 1 oz. orange juice

 1 dash bitters

 1 orange slice, halved (garnish)

GLASSWARE

 Rocks glass

1 Add the liquid ingredients to a pint glass filled with ice. Stir until thoroughly mixed.

2 Strain the resulting mixture into a rocks glass (with ice if desired).

3 Add an orange slice for garnish.

TETON TANYA

A contemporary spin on the classic Boulevardier, with Aperol and Cynar standing in for the traditional Campari and sweet vermouth, granting the drink a spicier, brighter quality.

INGREDIENTS

 1 oz. Aperol

 1 oz. Cynar

 1 oz. rye whiskey

 Splash Becherovka (garnish)

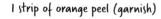 1 strip of orange peel (garnish)

GLASSWARE

 Rocks glass

1 Place all of the ingredients, except for the Becherovka and the garnish, in a mixing glass, fill it two-thirds of the way with ice, and stir until chilled.

2 Strain over a large ice cube into the rocks glass, garnish with the spritz of Becherovka and strip of orange peel, and enjoy.

IRISH SUNRISE

It's a bit unusual to see Irish whiskey mixed with fruity mixers, but the Irish Sunrise defies convention. This cocktail is sure to dazzle at any gathering and is the perfect choice to give your guests something new and exciting.

INGREDIENTS

 2 oz. Irish whiskey

 3 oz. lemon-lime soda

 Juice of 1 lemon wedge

 Juice of 1 lime wedge

 1 part grenadine

 1 lime wedge (garnish)

GLASSWARE
 Rocks glass

1 Add the whiskey and lemon-lime soda to your glass over ice.

2 Squeeze the juice of 1 lime wedge and 1 lemon wedge into the drink, and then top it with grenadine. Stir until thoroughly mixed.

3 Garnish with another lime wedge and enjoy!

RISIN' OUTLAW

This cross between an Old Fashioned and a Manhattan is dangerously good.

INGREDIENTS

1 oz. bourbon

1 oz. Del Maguey Vida mezcal

½ oz. Cocchi Americano

½ oz. Dolin dry vermouth

⅛ oz. Demerara syrup

⅛ oz. water

7 drops orange bitters

Lemon peel (garnish)

GLASSWARE
Rocks glass

1 Fill a rocks glass with ice and build the drink in it, adding the ingredients, except for the garnish, in the order they are listed.

2 Gently stir until chilled and garnish very lightly by squeezing the lemon peel over the drink and discard the peel.

BLACK PHILIP

This is one for those who want to live deliciously. With a blend of bitterness and sweetness, this drink is a smooth ride start to finish.

INGREDIENTS

1¾ oz. bourbon

¾ oz. Averna Amaro

¼ oz. Strega

2 dashes Peychaud's bitters

1 strip orange peel (garnish)

GLASSWARE

Rocks glass

1 Place all of the ingredients in a mixing glass, except for the garnish, fill it two-thirds of the way with ice, and stir until chilled.

2 Strain over ice into a rocks glass and garnish with the strip of orange peel.

ALL TAI'D UP

The concept is simple: make a Mai Tai but with bourbon. The result is delicious—a smoky, fruity, nutty cocktail that takes a classic recipe and elevates it into something new. The use of falernum gives the drink a little extra sweetness, and the flavor of the pecan really shines through. It's an unusual—but welcome—complement to the drink's classic orange and lime flavors.

INGREDIENTS

 1 banana leaf

 2 oz. bourbon

 1 oz. falernum

 ½ oz. orange juice

 ½ oz. lime juice

 ½ oz. curaçao

 1 lime slice (garnish)

 1 edible flower (garnish)

 1 mint sprig (garnish)

GLASSWARE
 Rocks glass

1 Trim the banana leaf into a rectangle and place it on the bottom of the rocks glass. Fill the glass with pebble ice.

2 Combine the remaining ingredients in a cocktail shaker, fill it two-thirds of the way with ice, and shake until chilled.

3 Strain the cocktail over ice into the glass, garnish with the lime slice, edible flower, and mint, and enjoy.

RENEGADE LEMONADE

It's a simple recipe, but sometimes the simplest drinks are the most satisfying. You'll quickly find yourself going back for seconds of this creation by Shane Carley.

INGREDIENTS

 I cup simple syrup (see page 7)

 Juice of 6 lemons

 I cup whiskey

 4 cups cold water

 I mint sprig (garnish)

 2 to 3 lemon slices (garnish)

GLASSWARE

 Mason jar

1. Add ice and the simple syrup to a half-gallon pitcher. Add the lemon juice and whiskey, and top off the mixture with water. Stir until thoroughly mixed.

2. Pour the drink into four Mason jars and garnish with sprigs of mint and a few lemon slices both inside and outside the jars.

RENEGADE SWEET TEA

The American South is known for its rebellious spirit, but it's also known for its undying love of sweet tea. This cocktail takes the latter and spikes it with a generous dose of the former, in the form of fine Kentucky bourbon. Of course, sweet tea will always be better if you brew it yourself, but for the sake of convenience, you can certainly use store-bought in this cocktail. You'll be bucking convention, but when you think about it, that's a little rebellious in itself.

INGREDIENTS

 4 oz. iced sweet tea

 1 oz. bourbon

 Sugar, to taste

 1 dash bitters

 1 lemon slice (garnish)

GLASSWARE

 Pint glass

1 If you plan to brew your own tea, be sure to do so several hours ahead of time so the tea has time to cool.

2 Add sweet tea and bourbon to a pint glass filled with ice. Stir in sugar until it reaches your desired level of sweetness.

3 Finish with a dash of bitters and garnish with a lemon slice.

SUMMER HONEY

Refreshing and full of summer fruit flavor, this is the ideal drink to sip while laying poolside.

INGREDIENTS

 1 oz. Jack Daniel's Tennessee Honey whiskey

 ½ oz. Midori

 1 oz. pineapple juice

 3 oz. lemon-lime soda

 orange slice, halved (garnish)

GLASSWARE

 Rocks glass

1 Place all of the ingredients, except for the soda and garnish, in a cocktail shaker, fill it two-thirds of the way with ice, and shake until chilled.

2 Add the soda, strain over ice into a glass, garnish with the orange slice, and enjoy.

SOUTHERN CHARM

This refreshing cucumber and watermelon cooler is just the thing to sip during hot Southern summers.

INGREDIENTS

 3 1" x 1" cubes of watermelon

 1 oz. Monin watermelon syrup

 2 oz. Four Roses bourbon

 8 mint leaves , plus extra for garnish

 4 to 5 drops Bittermens Hopped Grapefruit Bitters

 ½ oz. Pama (pomegranate liqueur)

 ½ oz. lime juice

 3 cucumber slices

 1 oz. Mr. Q Cumber sparkling cucumber beverage

GLASSWARE
 Rocks glass

1   In a shaker tin, muddle the three watermelon cubes and pour off the excess juice.

2   Add the remaining liquid ingredients.

3   Shake the ingredients and double strain the mixture into a glass over crushed ice.

4   Muddle the cucumber slices in a separate dry tin with the cucumber soda.

5   Shake and double strain the cucumber mixture to top the cocktail.

6   Garnish with mint and enjoy!

SPICED PUNCH

Bowl over the crowd at your holiday party with this refreshing and festive chai-spiced punch.

INGREDIENTS

 6 lemons, plus extra for garnish

 1 cup sugar

 4 cups water

 8 chai tea bags

 1 cup Four Roses bourbon

 1 12-oz. can ginger beer

 Cinnamon sticks (garnish)

 Cloves (garnish)

 Star anise (garnish)

 Allspice (garnish)

GLASSWARE

 Pitcher and glasses

1. Peel six lemons with a potato peeler and set peeled lemons aside. Put lemon peels and sugar in a bowl and crush peels into sugar. Allow to sit for one hour.

2. Juice the peeled lemons and strain juice to remove pulp.

3. Brew eight chai tea bags in four cups water. discard bags after use. Dissolve sugar and lemon peel mixture in chai tea while warm. Remove peels and discard. Add bourbon and juice from lemons. Chill in refrigerator.

4. Before serving, add one can ginger beer. Garnish with lemon slices and assorted spices floating in punch.

KENTUCKY MAID

The Kentucky Maid was created to celebrate the opening of SIDEBAR at Whiskey Row in 2013, which coincided with the Kentucky Derby. Naturally, it takes its inspiration from the traditional Derby cocktail, the mint julep. We recommend using Willet Bourbon.

INGREDIENTS

 2 English cucumber slices

 2 oz. bourbon

 6 mint leaves

 3/4 oz. lime juice

 3/4 oz. simple syrup (see page 7)

 1 English cucumber slice (garnish)

 1 mint sprig (garnish)

GLASSWARE

 Rocks glass

1 Muddle cucumber in cocktail shaker.

2 Place all of the ingredients, except for the garnish, in cocktail shaker, fill it two-thirds of the way with ice, and shake until chilled.

3 Strain over ice into a glass, garnish with a slice of cucumber with a sprig of mint stuck through the center, and enjoy.

THE O.G. O.F.

Full of warm spices and notes of caramel from the Demerara syrup, this aromatic Old Fashioned cocktail is best enjoyed on chilly winter nights.

INGREDIENTS

 2 oz. bourbon

 ¼ oz. Cocktail & Sons Spiced Demerara syrup

 2 dashes Angostura bitters

 2 drops Bittermans ole bitters

 Flamed orange twist (garnish)

GLASSWARE

 Rocks glass

1 Stir all ingredients except garnish with ice and strain into chilled glass. Garnish with a flamed orange twist.

LITTLE ITALY

Fans of the Manhattan will want to give this one a go, as the spicy richness of the Cynar is lovely beside the rye.

INGREDIENTS

 2 oz. rye whiskey

 ½ oz. Cynar

 ¾ oz. sweet vermouth

 2 maraschino cherries (garnish)

GLASSWARE
 Coupe (chilled)

1 Chill a coupe glass in the freezer.

2 Place the rye, Cynar, and vermouth in a mixing glass, fill it two-thirds of the way with ice, and stir until chilled.

3 Strain into the chilled glass and garnish with the cherries.

MILA'S SIGNATURE COCKTAIL

Developed by whiskey lover and Jim Beam brand ambassador Mila Kunis, this refreshing cocktail is the perfect balance of sweet vanilla and tart grapefruit.

INGREDIENTS

 1 oz. Jim Beam Vanilla bourbon whiskey

 2 oz. grapefruit juice

 1 oz. club soda

 Grapefruit slice, halved (garnish)

GLASSWARE
 Collins glass

1   Combine ingredients over ice and stir. Garnish with the grapefruit slice.

SUMMER CITRUS

Honeyed citrus with a hint of bitters makes this cocktail an excellent pick-me-up after a long day in the sun. We recommend using Four Roses Yellow Label Bourbon.

INGREDIENTS

 1¼ oz. bourbon

 ¾ oz. clover honey syrup (equal parts honey mixed with hot water)

 ½ oz. lemon juice

 ½ oz. grapefruit juice

 1 dash Angostura bitters, or to taste

 1 lemon twist (garnish)

GLASSWARE
 Rocks glass

1   Place all of the ingredients, except for the garnish, in a cocktail shaker, fill it two-thirds of the way with ice, and shake until chilled.

2   Strain over ice into a glass, garnish with the lemon twist, and enjoy.

COFFEE OLD FASHIONED

Irish Coffee (see page 48) is a beloved drink, but coffee works well with other whiskey drinks too. In this cocktail, coffee takes the place of vermouth in a classic Old Fashioned, creating a slightly bitter, slightly sweet alternative cocktail that is bursting with creativity!

INGREDIENTS

 I splash simple syrup (see page 7)

 I dash bitters

 I oz. whiskey

 2 oz. coffee

 Several coffee beans (garnish)

GLASSWARE

 Rocks glass

1 Add simple syrup and bitters to a rocks glass.

2 If using iced coffee, add ice.

3 Add whiskey and coffee.

4 Stir thoroughly.

5 Top with a few coffee beans.

CINNAMON APPLE

Whether in an apple pie or an apple crumble, few flavors go together more perfectly than cinnamon and apple. It might even be called the quintessential flavor of our land. After all, what's more American than apple pie? But pies are work and take time. Why spend the whole day preparing an apple pie when you can drink one instead? The Cinnamon Apple cocktail, developed by Shane Carley, features the delicious flavors you expect from your favorite homemade treats but with a delightful buzz in lieu of the sugar rush.

INGREDIENTS

 2 oz. apple cider

 1 oz. apple liqueur

 1 oz. cinnamon whiskey

 1 cinnamon stick (garnish)

 1 apple slice (garnish)

GLASSWARE
 Rocks glass

1 Fill a rocks glass with ice and add the cider, apple liqueur, and cinnamon whiskey. Stir until thoroughly mixed.

2 Garnish with a cinnamon stick and apple slice and enjoy!

HOT BUTTERED BOURBON

This rich bourbon variation of Hot Buttered Rum will be your new wintertime favorite.

INGREDIENTS

 1 1/2 oz. bourbon

 1 oz. (or 1 heaping dessert spoon) Hot Buttered Rum mix

 1 dash Angostura bitters

 Very hot water

 Grated nutmeg or a cinnamon stick (garnish)

GLASSWARE

 Glass mug

1   Fill mug up to the top with hot water and allow to temper for 45 seconds.

2   Dump hot water and refill to 2/3 with hot water. Add a heaping dessert spoon of Hot Buttered Rum mix and stir vigorously.

3   Add Four Roses Bourbon and one dash of Angostura bitters. Top with more hot water if needed and give a quick stir.

4   Garnish with grated nutmeg or a cinnamon stick, and serve with the spoon in.

HOT BUTTERED RUM MIX

1 lb. room temperature butter

6 cups brown sugar

4 teaspoons ground cinnamon

2 teaspoons grated nutmeg

1 teaspoon ground cloves

1 teaspoon kosher salt

1 Combine and stir until evenly mixed. Pour into a glass and enjoy.

HOT APPLE CIDER

This recipe for spiked cider makes enough for fifteen servings and has the added benefit of filling your home with the gorgeous scent of spices, apple, and orange.

INGREDIENTS

 2 oz. apple cider (2 liters)

 1 oz. bourbon (1 liter)

 5 cinnamon sticks

 3 oranges (garnish)

 30 to 40 cloves (garnish)

GLASSWARE

 Glass mug

1 Put the apple cider and the Four Roses Yellow Label in a slow-cooker or on the stove on low for two hours before guests arrive.

2 Add cinnamon sticks, making sure the liquid is not boiling (this can bring out bitter/woody notes from the cinnamon).

3 Peel 2½" x 1" sections of the oranges, poke in cloves, and garnish each cocktail with a clove-studded orange peel.

MISH MASH

Ever forget to restock your liquor cabinet for a few weeks, or maybe even months? Once in a while, you open the cabinet and realize you're left with just a handful of odds and ends that don't really make anything. The Mish Mash takes a couple odds and ends you likely always have mixes in a bit of bourbon, and gives you a surprisingly delicious result.

INGREDIENTS

 2 oz. bourbon

 1 oz. triple sec

 1 oz. simple syrup (see page 7)

 1 splash grenadine

 Orange peel (garnish)

GLASSWARE

 Rocks glass

1 Fill a glass with ice and add bourbon, triple sec, and simple syrup.

2 Stir together until mixed. Top with a splash of grenadine and, if desired, a lemon peel.

APPLE SANGRIA

Full of crisp autumnal flavors, this take on sangria is perfect for raising a glass to the changing seasons. We recommend using Jack Daniel's Single Barrel.

INGREDIENTS

2 oz. chardonnay (low-oak)

1/3 oz. bourbon or Tennessee whiskey

1/3 oz. apple brandy

1 oz. apple cider

1/3 oz. honey

Sliced ginger, to taste

Cinnamon sticks

Juice of 1 lime

Juice of 1 lemon

Diced apples (garnish)

Lemon slices (garnish)

GLASSWARE
Pitcher and glasses

1   Combine all ingredients except for the garnish in a pitcher and refrigerate. Before serving, add the diced apples and citrus and mix well.

AUTUMN LEAVES

This aromatic, spirit-forward cocktail is just the thing to warm up cool autumn evenings.

INGREDIENTS

1¼ oz. bourbon

¼ oz. Carpano Antica Formula

½ oz. Amaro Ramazzotti

1 dash Angostura bitters

Lemon peel (garnish)

GLASSWARE
Rocks glass

1 Add all ingredients to a mixing glass and stir. Pour into a double rocks glass over fresh ice. Garnish by squeezing the lemon peel over the drink and discard the peel.

PUNCH 415

This punch takes its name from U. police code 415—disturbing the peace. This is definitely the cocktail to have on hand for big, raucous celebrations. We recommend using Four Roses Single Barrel Bourbon.

INGREDIENTS

 1½ oz. bourbon

 ¾ oz. lime juice

 ½ oz. Monin Almond (orgeat) syrup

 2 oz. pineapple juice

 5 dashes Angostura bitters

 1 mint sprig (garnish)

GLASSWARE
Rocks glass

1 Place all of the ingredients, except for the garnish, in a cocktail shaker, fill it two-thirds of the way with ice, and shake until chilled.

2 Strain over ice into a glass, garnish with the fresh mint, and enjoy.

SOPHISTICATED SIPPERS

By the very nature of the careful process of its creation, whiskey has a real distinction, and sometimes you want to lean in to its grand stature and enjoy a drink with some sophistication. Find something bubbly like Love & Happiness, something darker and more complex like the Sunday Nightcap, something smoky and citrusy like the Select and Stave, and everything in between. If you want something classy and delicious, look no further.

INNUENDO

Corsair's complex Triple Smoke Whiskey blends beautifully with the tea and fruit flavors in this cocktail. A perfect drink for anyone who enjoys a cup of Lapsang souchong.

INGREDIENTS

 2 oz. Corsair Triple Smoke American Single Malt Whiskey

 1 oz. tea

 ¾ oz. peach simple syrup

 ¼ oz. lemon juice

 Lemon peel (garnish)

 GLASSWARE
Rocks glass

1 Place all of the ingredients, except for the garnish, in a cocktail shaker, fill it two-thirds of the way with ice, and shake until chilled.

2 Strain over ice into a rocks glass, garnish with the lemon peel, and enjoy.

BLACK FORREST

A decidedly grown-up drink, the Black Forrest complements the Triple Smoke with Hünerkopf Alt, a rich German half-bitter with aromas of orange rind, allspice, and brandied cherries.

INGREDIENTS

 2 oz. Corsair Triple Smoke American Single Malt Whiskey

 ½ oz. Hünerkopf Alt German half-bitter

 ¼ oz. sorghum syrup (2:1 sorghum to water)

 1 pinch salt

 Lemon peel (garnish)

GLASSWARE
 Snifter

1. Place all of the ingredients, except for the garnish, in a mixing glass, fill it two-thirds of the way with ice, and stir until chilled.

2. Strain into a snifter, garnish with the lemon peel, and enjoy.

THOMPSON'S OLD FASHIONED

Supremely versatile, the Old Fashioned formula works with just about any whiskey—and indeed, almost any spirit. Named for Thompson Willett, founder of the original Willett Distillery, this Old Fashioned gets a kick from Willett Family Estate Rye but is equally good when made with their Pure Kentucky Small Batch or Noah's Mill bourbons. We encourage you to try them all.

INGREDIENTS

 1 oz. simple syrup (see page 7)

 3 to 4 shakes bitters

 2 oz. Willett Family Estate Bottled Rye

 Water or club soda (optional)

 Luxardo cherries (garnish)

 Orange (garnish)

GLASSWARE
 Rocks glass

1   Combine simple syrup and bitters in a tumbler. Top with ice and fill with rye. Leave a little room for water or club soda if desired.

2   Drop in one or two Luxardo cherries and rub the orange wedge around the rim of the glass. Enjoy!

PREAKNESS

Bénédictine gives this Manhattan-inspired cocktail a sweet, herbal twist.

INGREDIENTS

 2 oz. rye whiskey

 ½ oz. Bénédictine

 ½ oz. sweet vermouth

 2 dashes Angostura bitters

GLASSWARE

 Rocks glass

1 Place all of the ingredients in a cocktail shaker, fill it two-thirds of the way with ice, and shake until chilled.

2 Strain into a rocks glass and enjoy.

FALCON SMASH

Sweet basil and Corsair's peppery Ryemageddon make an ace combination in this smash cocktail.

INGREDIENTS

 2 oz. Corsair Ryemageddon rye whiskey

 1 oz. lemon juice

 6 basil leaves

 1 oz. simple syrup (see page 7)

 Basil (garnish)

 GLASSWARE
Rocks glass

1 Combine all the ingredients in a rocks glass. Gently muddle basil and top with ice. Garnish with one or two additional basil leaves.

LOVE & HAPPINESS

This classy, refreshing, and complex serve is a tribute to one of Al Green's very best songs.

INGREDIENTS

 2 oz. single malt whiskey

 1 oz. Amaro Averna

 2 oz. dry sparkling wine

GLASSWARE

 Champagne flute

1 Chill a champagne flute in the freezer.

2 Place the whiskey and amaro in a mixing glass, fill it two-thirds of the way with ice, and stir until chilled.

3 Strain into the chilled champagne flute and top with the sparkling wine.

MR. SMOOTH

This is a riff on the Vieux Carré (see page 36), a classic New Orleans cocktail that was created at the famous Carousel Bar in the Monteleone Hotel. Between the bourbon, Cynar, and Demerara syrup, there are plenty of luscious caramel notes to enjoy, proof that the moniker is not just a clever nickname.

INGREDIENTS

 2 oz. bourbon

 ¼ oz. Cognac

 ¼ oz. Cynar

 ¼ oz. Demerara syrup

 2 dashes Angostura bitters

 Mint leaves (garnish)

GLASSWARE

 Highball glass

1 Place all of the ingredients in a mixing glass, fill it two-thirds of the way with ice, and stir until chilled.

2 Strain the cocktail into the highball glass, garnish with the mint leaves, and enjoy.

SLIPPING INTO DARKNESS

This one is both rich and light but packs a surprising punch.

INGREDIENTS

 1½ oz. rye whiskey

 4 oz. root beer

 3 dashes absinthe

 1 lemon wedge (garnish)

GLASSWARE
 Highball glass

1 Add all the ingredients to a highball glass filled with ice, stir until chilled, and garnish with the lemon wedge.

HIJINKS

As fans of single malt Scotch tend toward excessive seriousness when it comes to their preferred spirit, it falls to the rest of us to get them to lighten up and think outside the box. They will no doubt recoil when you first suggest mixing Scotch into a cocktail, but upon encountering the delicate floral aromas that the Hijinks unlocks, they will no doubt undergo an attitude adjustment.

INGREDIENTS

 1½ oz. X by Glenmorangie single malt scotch whisky

 ¾ oz. Lustau Fino Jarana sherry

 ¾ oz. chamomile syrup

 ½ oz. lemon juice

 1 dehydrated lemon slice (garnish)

 GLASSWARE
Coupe

1 Place all of the ingredients , except for the garnish, in a cocktail shaker, fill it two-thirds of the way with ice, and shake until chilled.

2 Strain the cocktail into the coupe, garnish with the dehydrated lemon slice, and enjoy.

MARGOT TENENBAUM

The Rabarbaro Zucca Amaro makes this cocktail as enigmatic as it is brilliant.

INGREDIENTS

2 oz. bourbon

3/4 oz. lemon juice

1/2 oz. honey syrup (equal parts honey and hot water)

1/2 oz. Rabarbaro Zucca Amaro

GLASSWARE

Rocks glass

1 Place all of the ingredients in a cocktail shaker, fill it two-thirds of the way with ice, and shake until chilled.

2 Strain over one large ice cube into a rocks glass.

FOUR ROSES HOT TODDY

Another delicious seasonal cocktail, this winter warmer was created by Four Roses way back in 1943.

INGREDIENTS

 I sugar cube

 Hot water

 Lemon peel

 Cloves

 I cinnamon stick (optional)

 1½ oz. bourbon or rye whiskey

GLASSWARE
 Pitcher and mugs

1 Place a cube of sugar in the bottom of the glass and dissolve with a little hot water.

2 Add twist of lemon peel (bruise firmly), four cloves and, and if you desire, a stick of cinnamon.

3 Pour a generous jigger of Four Roses Bourbon into your mug.

4 Fill the glass with steaming hot water. Enjoy!

BUFFALO SMASH

Strictly speaking, every smash is a julep, but a julep isn't always a smash (much like all bourbon is whiskey, but the opposite isn't necessarily true). The key difference is that a smash can use herbs other than mint and usually brings lemon and seasonal fruit into the mix—in this case, ripe blackberries. We recommend using Buffalo Trace Bourbon.

INGREDIENTS

 2 blackberries

 6 to 8 mint leaves , plus extra for garnish

 ½ oz. honey syrup (equal parts honey and hot water)

 1 oz. lemon juice

 3 oz. bourbon

 Soda water, to finish

 Blackberries (garnish)

GLASSWARE
 Rocks glass

1 "Smash" (muddle) 2 blackberries, and 6–8 mint leaves with honey syrup in shaker tin.

2 Add lemon juice and bourbon to shaker tin. Shake vigorously with cracked ice.

3 Double-strain into cocktail glass with fresh crushed ice.

4 Top with soda water and garnish with blackberry and mint sprig.

THIRD COAST MULE

Coastal areas in the US that are neither East Coast nor West Coast are sometimes referred to by the somewhat tongue-in-cheek moniker "Third Coast." Houston's location on the Gulf of Mexico certainly qualifies, and this cheekily named cocktail brings a whole mess of Texas flavor. Yellow Rose Distilling was Houston's first legal whiskey distillery, and it makes sense to honor that heritage with a Texas-sized twist on an old classic.

INGREDIENTS

 1½ oz. whiskey

 ¾ oz. lemon juice

 ¾ oz. simple syrup (see page 7)

 ½ oz. coconut water

 1½ oz. ginger beer

 1 strip lemon peel (garnish)

GLASSWARE

 Collins glass

1 Place the whiskey, lemon juice, and syrup in a cocktail shaker, fill it two-thirds of the way with ice, and shake until chilled.

2 Strain over ice into the Collins glass and top with the coconut water and ginger beer.

3 Express the strip of lemon peel over the cocktail, garnish the drink with it, and enjoy.

SUNDAY NIGHTCAP

You're probably familiar with the Sunday Scaries even if you don't know them by name. It's the feeling you get at the end of the weekend when you start to dread your reentry into the real world, when that pit forms in your stomach and your thoughts drift toward all the work that lies ahead of you this week. This drink will help you forget. With its balance of sweet and bitter flavors, this play on a Boulevardier is the perfect beverage to grab your full attention and refocus your thoughts on relaxation and enjoyment. Substituting red wine in place of the usual sweet vermouth adds a drier, richer character to the drink and lends it a darker, more inky complexion.

INGREDIENTS

1 oz. rye whiskey

1 oz. Campari

1 oz. red wine

1 orange twist (garnish)

GLASSWARE

Rocks glass

1 Add the whiskey, Campari, and wine to a pint glass filled with ice. Stir thoroughly.

2 Strain the resulting mixture into a rocks glass filled with ice.

3 Garnish with an orange twist.

DOOMSDAY CLOCK

Whiskey and ginger are two flavors that play off one another well, as the bite of ginger stands up to the strong flavor of the spirit. The Doomsday Clock is a dark, boozy cocktail that lets the competing flavors of its primary ingredients stand on their own. The addition of simple syrup and bitters gives it another sweet yet spicy element and lends a surprising depth of flavor to the drink.

INGREDIENTS

 2 oz. whiskey

 1 dash bitters

 1 dash simple syrup (see page 7)

 1 oz. ginger beer

 GLASSWARE
Rocks glass

1   Stir the whiskey, bitters, and simple syrup together in a rocks glass with ice.

2   Top with ginger beer.

CUCUMBER JULEP

The Mint Julep is a classic cocktail, but it's heavy on bourbon and not much else. The Cucumber Julep elevates it using the freshness of cucumber, adding a crisp flavor complemented well by the addition of a small amount of club soda. Mint Julep purists might turn up their noses at the Cucumber Julep, but those looking for the perfect accompaniment to a vegetarian meal will find a friend in this creative take on an old favorite.

INGREDIENTS

 6 mint leaves

 6 cucumber slices

 1 splash simple syrup (see page 7)

 2 oz. bourbon

 ½ oz. club soda

 1 cucumber swizzle (garnish)

 1 mint sprig (garnish)

GLASSWARE
 Lowball glass or mint julep glass

1 In a cocktail shaker, muddle the mint leaves and cucumber slices with the simple syrup.

2 Fill the cocktail shaker with ice and add the bourbon. Shake well.

3 Strain the resulting mixture into a lowball glass filled with ice.

4 Top with club soda.

5 Garnish with a cucumber swizzle and a mint sprig.

OLD KENTUCKY ROAD

When you want to feel classy, a few cocktails immediately come to mind: the Old Fashioned, the Martini, the Manhattan. Those drinks share an important quality: simplicity. The classiest cocktails are often the easiest to make because they are made with the goal of coaxing the most flavor out of the fewest ingredients. The Old Kentucky Road continues this tradition, balancing the oaky richness of bourbon with the refreshing sweetness of ginger ale, with just a hint of mint and lime to round out the flavor of this delicate and refined cocktail.

INGREDIENTS

 2 mint leaves

 1 splash lime juice

 2 oz. bourbon whiskey

 1 oz. ginger ale

 1 lime wedge (garnish)

 1 mint leaf (garnish)

 GLASSWARE:
Rocks glass

1 Muddle the mint leaves and lime juice in the bottom of a cocktail shaker.

2 Fill the cocktail shaker with ice and add the bourbon. Shake well.

3 Strain the resulting mixture into a rocks glass filled with ice.

4 Top with ginger ale. Lightly stir if desired.

5 Garnish with a lime wedge and mint leaf.

SILVER 75

This bourbon rendition of the French 75 takes its name from The Silver Dollar, a honky tonk joint in downtown Louisville, named one of the best whiskey bars by both *GQ* and Thrillist.

INGREDIENTS

¾ oz. bourbon

½ oz. simple syrup (see page 7)

½ oz. lemon juice

4 oz. sparkling wine

Lemon peel (garnish)

GLASSWARE

Wine glass or coupe

1 Combine bourbon, lemon, and simple syrup in a tin and shake very lightly.

2 Strain into a wine glass or coupe with ice and top with sparkling wine.

3 Garnish with a lemon peel expressed and set on top of the cocktail.

JAM SESSION

Whiskey doesn't get enough credit for how well it pairs with fruit liqueurs, particularly dark ones. Cherry, blackberry, and other berry liqueurs make a nice sweet accompaniment to the often smoky, sometimes harsh bite of the whiskey. This simple rye whiskey cocktail evokes blackberry jam, resulting in the perfect drink to wind down with at the end of a long day.

INGREDIENTS

 2 oz. rye whiskey

 1 oz. blackberry liqueur

 1 dash simple syrup (see page 7)

 1 dash lemon juice

 1 lemon twist (garnish)

GLASSWARE

 Rocks glass

1 Place all of the ingredients, except for the garnish, in a cocktail shaker, fill it two-thirds of the way with ice, and shake until chilled.

2 Strain over ice into a rocks glass, garnish with the lemon twist, and enjoy.

ELDER SHAMROCK

If you're anything like us, the first thing you reach for on St. Patrick's Day is probably a pint of Guinness. But if you want something a little more refined, the Elder Shamrock will do the trick. It makes a compelling case for keeping elderflower liqueur on hand, as its floral sweetness does a great job offsetting the bite of Irish whiskey. This is the perfect drink for quietly sipping at home when you don't feel like heading out to a bar.

INGREDIENTS

 2 oz. Irish whiskey

 1 oz. elderflower liqueur

 1 oz. lemon juice

 1 lemon twist (garnish)

GLASSWARE

 Rocks glass

1 Add the whiskey, elderflower liqueur, and lemon juice to a mixing glass filled with ice. Stir thoroughly.

2 Strain the resulting mixture into a rocks glass filled with ice.

3 Garnish with a twist of lemon.

FOND FAREWELL

Not all reasons to drink are happy ones, but drinking when you're sad isn't always unhealthy. No, you don't want to fall into the trap of "drowning your sorrows" in alcohol, but a toast to the dearly departed is often appropriate and appreciated. The Fond Farewell is a simple whiskey cocktail that feels solemn, austere, and serious—a fitting tribute to any recently passed friend, family member, or even beloved pet.

INGREDIENTS

2 oz. bourbon

1 oz. amaretto

Juice of 1 orange slice

1 orange twist (garnish)

GLASSWARE

Rocks glass

1 Add the bourbon and amaretto to a mixing glass filled with ice. Squeeze in the juice from one orange slice and stir until thoroughly mixed.

2 Strain the resulting mixture into a rocks glass filled with ice.

3 Garnish with a twist of orange.

GENTLEMAN'S MANHATTAN

This variation on the Manhattan swaps out the traditional rye whiskey for the smoother Gentleman Jack.

INGREDIENTS

 2 oz. Gentleman Jack whiskey

 1/2 oz. sweet vermouth

 1/2 oz. dry vermouth

 2 dashes bitters

 1 maraschino cherry (garnish)

 1 lemon twist (garnish)

 GLASSWARE
Coupe or cocktail glass

1 Place all of the ingredients, except for the garnish, in a cocktail shaker, fill it two-thirds of the way with ice, and shake until chilled.

2 Strain into a coupe or cocktail glass,, garnish with the cherry and twist of orange, and enjoy.

SELECT AND STAVE

Sweet, smoky, and citrus flavors balance one another perfectly in this Jack Daniel's creation. We recommend using Jack Daniel's Single Barrel Select as your whiskey.

INGREDIENTS

1 oz. Tennessee whiskey

¾ oz. sweet vermouth

¾ oz. Cherry Heering

1 oz. orange juice

GLASSWARE
Cocktail glass

1 Place all of the ingredients, except for the orange juice, in a cocktail shaker, fill it two-thirds of the way with ice, and shake until chilled.

2 Strain the mixture into a chilled martini glass and top with orange juice.

OLD AS DIRT

This excellent riff on the Old Fashioned uses Corsair Quinoa Whiskey, one of the distillery's signature madcap inventions.

INGREDIENTS

 2 oz. Corsair Quinoa Whiskey

 ½ oz. honey syrup (equal parts honey and hot water)

 1 dash Angostura bitters

 1 orange slice (garnish)

GLASSWARE
 Rocks glass

1 Combine all the ingredients, except for the garnish, in a rocks glass with ice and stir.

2 Garnish with orange slice and serve.

DARK SIDE

This original creation from the minds at Hartfield & Co. balances the rich flavors of whiskey and Bonal with a one-two citrus punch of lime juice and orange bitters. We recommend using Hartfield & Co. American Whiskey.

INGREDIENTS

2 oz. American whiskey

¾ oz. simple syrup (see page 7)

1 oz. Bonal

¾ oz. lime juice

7 dashes Regan's orange bitters

1 lime slice (garnish)

GLASSWARE

Collins glass

1 Place all of the ingredients, except for the garnish, in a cocktail shaker, fill it two-thirds of the way with ice, and shake until chilled.

2 Strain over ice into a Collins glass, garnish with the lime slice, and enjoy.

WHALEN SMASH

Whiskey and ginger is a time-honored flavor combination, but precious few whiskey cocktails do an adequate job including mint. The Whalen Smash forgoes the ginger liqueurs that similar cocktails often call for, instead adding a splash of ginger beer to give the drink some added lightness. The carbonation gives the drink a playful element but doesn't overwhelm the palate, leaving plenty of room for the mint and lemon to play off one another.

INGREDIENTS

 ½ lemon, cut into wedges

 4 mint leaves

 3 oz. bourbon

 1 oz. ginger beer

 Lemon or lime slices (garnish)

GLASSWARE

 Rocks glass or julep cup

1. Squeeze the lemon wedges into your rocks glass or julep cup, and drop the squeezed wedges into the glass.

2. Add the mint and muddle it with the lemon juice. Add ice as desired.

3. Pour the bourbon into the glass and top the mixture with a splash of ginger beer.

4. Stir the drink together, garnish it with citrus, and enjoy!

HOT TENNESSEE TODDY

Another great warmer for anyone feeling the winter chill, Jack Daniel's soothing and slightly spiced take on the hot toddy will cure what ails you.

INGREDIENTS

 1 oz. Jack Daniel's Tennessee whiskey

 1 spoonful honey

 1 cinnamon stick

 1 squeeze lemon juice

 Hot water

 1 lemon slice (garnish)

GLASSWARE
 Glass mug

1 Pour the Jack Daniel's into a heavy mug.

2 Add the honey, cinnamon stick, and lemon juice, and top the drink with hot water.

3 Stir the drink, garnish with a lemon slice, and serve.

MASON JAR BOURBON PRESS

A classic cocktail for whiskey lovers, the Bourbon Press is a perfect drink for anytime and anywhere. It's very much an outdoor drink, right down to its appearance: It looks like nothing so much as a glass of lemonade or iced tea. In this case, a drop or two of orange bitters will add a bit of a twist to this classic flavor combo. The Bourbon Press is the perfect drink to take to the park while you relax with a good book. Screw a lid on that Mason jar and head out there!

INGREDIENTS

 2 oz. bourbon

 1 dash orange bitters

 2 oz. ginger ale

 2 oz. club soda

 1 mint sprig (garnish)

 A slice of lemon (garnish)

GLASSWARE

 Mason jar

1 Add a few good-sized ice cubes to your Mason jar and pour in the bourbon.

2 Add a quick dash of orange bitters.

3 Fill the remainder of the glass with equal parts ginger ale and club soda.

4 Garnish the drink with mint and a slice of lemon and enjoy.

SOUR
SATISFACTION

The Whiskey Sour is one of the most iconic cocktails of all time. So iconic in fact that it has inspired the creation of dozens of other sours that play (and improve upon? You decide!) with the original concept. Some, like the South of NY Sour, take a spin that embraces spice, and others, like the Forth & Clyde, add in sweetness, bitterness, and heat to balance out the sour. All of these and other cocktails that celebrate that essential sour sensation can be found in this chapter.

WHISKEY SOUR

Ah yes, the famous Whiskey Sour. Made a variety of different ways, sometimes with egg whites, sometimes with sour mix, and sometimes simply with lemon juice. The drink is as sour as its name implies, adding an unexpected new dimension to the whiskey. Smashing whiskey and lemon juice together head-on, this delicious, classic concoction is what comes out of the wreckage.

INGREDIENTS

 2½ oz. rye whiskey

 1 oz. lemon juice

 ⅓ oz. simple syrup (see page 7)

 1 maraschino cherry (garnish)

 1 orange slice, halved (garnish)

 GLASSWARE
Rocks glass

1 Place all of the ingredients, except for the garnish, in a cocktail shaker, fill it two-thirds of the way with ice, and shake until chilled.

2 Strain over ice into a glass, garnish with the maraschino cherry and orange slice, and enjoy.

BUDGET SOUR

One of the great things about living in the modern age is convenience. There are microwave dinners and smartphones, and anyone who doesn't feel like mixing a cocktail can go out and buy a mix to make their lives easier. As far as mixes go, sour mix is probably one of the more popular options and makes the Budget Sour a convenient, hassle-free alternative to the traditional Whiskey Sour.

INGREDIENTS

 1 oz. rye whiskey

 2 oz. sour mix

 1 lemon slice, quartered (garnish)

GLASSWARE

 Rocks glass

1 Add the whiskey and sour mix to a rocks glass filled with ice. Stir until thoroughly mixed.

2 Garnish with a lemon slice.

NEW YORK SOUR

Aficionados may find it hard to believe, but The Famous Grouse is the number one whisky in Scotland, the mecca of whisky. Its soft and sweet taste makes it a natural for cocktails.

INGREDIENTS

 2 oz. The Famous Grouse Scotch whisky

 ¾ oz. simple syrup (see page 7)

 ¾ oz. lemon juice

 ¼ oz. dry red wine

 1 lemon slice (garnish)

 1 brandy-soaked cherry (garnish)

GLASSWARE

 Rocks glass

1 Place the Scotch, simple syrup, and lemon juice in a cocktail shaker, fill it two-thirds of the way with ice, and shake until chilled.

2 Strain into a rocks glass filled with ice and float the wine on top by pouring it over the back of a spoon.

3 Garnish with the lemon slice and brandy-soaked cherry.

SOUTH OF NY SOUR

A Southern spin on the whiskey sour, this fantastic creation from Corsair has just the right amount of spice.

INGREDIENTS

 2 oz. Corsair Triple Smoke American Single Malt Whiskey

 1 oz. lemon juice

 1 oz. simple syrup (see page 7)

 1 egg white

 5 drops barbecue bitters

 1 oz. Malbec

 Pink peppercorns, cracked (garnish)

GLASSWARE
 Rocks glass

1. Combine whiskey, lemon juice, simple syrup, egg white, and bitters in a mixing tin without ice, and shake the tin to froth the egg.

2. Add ice and shake again.

3. Strain the mixture into a rocks glass with fresh ice.

4. Top with the Malbec and garnish with cracked pink peppercorns.

BOURBON WHISKEY SOUR

Delicious, a total breeze to make, and great for entertaining, the sour is a classic for good reason. This recipe is courtesy of Hartfield & Co. Bourbon.

INGREDIENTS

 2 oz. bourbon

 ³/₄ oz. simple syrup (see page 7)

 ³/₄ oz. lemon juice

 1 egg white

 1 lemon peel (garnish)

GLASSWARE

 Rocks glass

1 Build the drink in a shaker, dry shake (without ice), add ice, and shake again.

2 Double strain the drink into a double rocks glass over fresh ice.

3 Express oil from the lemon peel over the drink, garnish with the lemon peel, and serve.

FORTH & CLYDE

A delicate balance of bitter, sweet, sour, and heat dwells in the Forth & Clyde. That may seem like a lot to fit into one glass, but St-Germain, which is a master at making the complex seem a matter of course, is more than up to the task.

INGREDIENTS

 Honey, as needed

 Red pepper flakes, to taste

 1 oz. Maker's Mark bourbon

 1 oz. Hendrick's gin

 1 oz. St-Germain

 1 oz. lime juice

GLASSWARE

 Rocks glass

1 Chill the cocktail glass in the freezer.

2 Pour a nickel-sized quantity of honey into a cocktail shaker.

3 Add red pepper flakes and the remaining ingredients and stir until the honey has dissolved.

4 Add as much ice as you can fit into the shaker, and shake for 18 seconds.

5 Strain the cocktail into the chilled rocks glass and enjoy.

BOURBON BENDER

A little like a sour, this Paul Knorr creation is great for summer picnics.

INGREDIENTS

 I oz. bourbon

 I oz. amaretto

 I oz. lime juice

GLASSWARE

 Rocks glass

1. Place all of the ingredients in a cocktail shaker, fill it two-thirds of the way with ice, and shake until chilled.

2. Strain into a glass and enjoy.

RYE SOUR

This drink is as sour as its name implies, adding an unexpected new dimension to the whiskey. The Whiskey Sour takes whiskey and lemon juice and smashes them together head on, creating this delicious, classic concoction.

INGREDIENTS

 2 ½ oz. rye whiskey

 1 oz. lemon juice

 ⅓ oz. simple syrup (see page 7)

 1 maraschino cherry (garnish)

 1 lemon slice, halved (garnish)

GLASSWARE

 Rocks glass

1 Place all of the ingredients, except for the garnish, in a cocktail shaker, fill it two-thirds of the way with ice, and shake until chilled.

2 Strain over ice into a glass, garnish with the maraschino cherry and lemon slice, and enjoy.

WINTER RYE SOUR

This spin on the classic Rye Sour (see page 223) is the perfect way to warm up in the winter. It brings all of the comfort of a relaxing tea, with the added kick of a good rye whiskey.

INGREDIENTS

 1 rosemary sprig

 1½ oz. honey syrup (equal parts honey and hot water)

 1 oz. rye whiskey

 1½ oz. lemon juice

 1 oz. egg white

 1 rosemary sprig (garnish)

GLASSWARE

 Rocks glass

1 Muddle the rosemary sprig and honey syrup in a shaker.

2 Add the liquid ingredients and egg white and dry shake (without ice).

3 Add ice and shake again before straining into a rocks glass. Garnish with the rosemary sprig and enjoy!

WATER FOR ELEPHANTS
RYE SWIZZLE

A classic Swizzle is a lot like a sour-style cocktail but mixed with a swizzle stick and served in a tall glass with lots of ice. Originally from the Caribbean and often made with rum, it's the ultimate summer cocktail. Willett's Rye Swizzle benefits from the herbal honeyed flavor of their Family Estate Small Batch Rye, with Tippleman's Double Spiced Falernum Syrup supplying an extra kick of ginger, clove, and lime zest.

INGREDIENTS

 1 to 2 oz. rye whiskey

 Juice of 1 lime

 3 to 4 dashes bitters

 1 oz. Tippleman's Double Spiced Falernum syrup

 1 lime wedge (garnish)

GLASSWARE

 Collins glass

1 Combine rye, lime juice, bitters, and syrup in Collins glass.

2 Top with ice, garnish with lime wedge, and swizzle.

WAX AND WANE

Basil, rosemary, and charred cedar lend a woodsy, herbal note to this sophisticated interpretation of a Whiskey Sour.

INGREDIENTS

 2 oz. rye whiskey

 ¼ oz. lemon juice

 ¼ oz. Demerara simple syrup

 4 dashes Angostura bitters

 1 egg white

 6 basil leaves

 1 rosemary sprig (garnish)

 1 cedar paper by Fire and Flavor (garnish)

GLASSWARE
 Collins glass

1 Place all of the ingredients, except for the garnish, in a cocktail shaker, fill it two-thirds of the way with ice, and shake until chilled.

2 Strain over ice into a collins glass.

3 Briefly (and carefully!) catch the cedar paper on fire, extinguish it, then add to it your drink with the rosemary sprig.

MASH EFFECT

What is sour mash? Excellent question! You've probably seen it on the side of some whiskey bottles. It's similar to sourdough bread: the fermentation of sour mash whiskey uses material from an older existing mash. So if you ever thought twice about buying sour mash whiskey because you were afraid it might have a sour flavor, never fear—that's not what it refers to. Now that you've learned a little something, here's a fun drink!

INGREDIENTS

 2 oz. sour mash whiskey

 1 oz. sweet vermouth

 1 oz. cherry cola

 2 brandy-soaked cherries (garnish)

GLASSWARE

 Rocks glass

1 Add ice to a rocks glass. Pour in the whiskey and vermouth.

2 Top with cherry cola.

3 Drop in the brandy-soaked cherries.

WHISKEY SUNSET

Whiskey is far from the easiest liquor to use in a summer sipper, but with a little white wine to take off the edge, the Whiskey Sunset succeeds admirably. The Whiskey Sunset incorporates a few extra sweet and sour notes to create a delicious and well-rounded concoction.

INGREDIENTS

 2 oz. bourbon

 2 oz. white wine

 1 oz. lemonade

 1 dash simple syrup (see page 7)

 3 oz. ginger ale

 1 lemon slice (garnish)

 1 orange slice (garnish)

GLASSWARE

 Mason jar

1 Fill your glass with ice and all the liquid ingredients except the ginger ale. Stir thoroughly, then top the drink with ginger ale.

2 Garnish with a lemon slice and orange slice and enjoy.

VANILLA FIZZ

This creamy, frothy confection is a Kentucky-style spin on the New Orleans Gin Fizz.

INGREDIENTS

 1 oz. bourbon

 2 oz. half-and-half

1 oz. lemon sour mix

 1 oz. egg white

 Club soda

Orange peel (garnish)

GLASSWARE
Collins glass

1 Combine all ingredients, except the club soda and garnish, in a shaker. Shake vigorously for as long as you can.

2 Strain into a chilled Collins glass and spritz with club soda (the egg whites will grow out of the glass). Garnish with an orange peel.

THUNDER PUNCH

Taking its inspiration from the Fuzzy Navel and the Moscow Mule, the Thunder Punch strikes the perfect balance of sweet and sour. We recommend using Four Roses Yellow Label Bourbon.

INGREDIENTS

Lemon slices

1½ oz. bourbon

½ oz. peach purée

½ oz. blood orange bitters
(Stirrings brand recommended)

¼ oz. lemon juice

1½ oz. ginger beer

GLASSWARE

Hurricane glass

1 Place the lemon slices in the bottom of a Hurricane glass and fill the glass with ice.

2 Add all the remaining ingredients, except for the ginger beer, into a shaker tin with ice.

3 Shake the mixture for 10 seconds, and strain it into a hurricane glass over ice.

4 Top the drink with ginger beer and serve.

KENTUCKY VANILLA DROP

This simple twist on the classic Lemon Drop cocktail balances tart lemon with creamy vanilla—a little like a lemon Creamsicle. Enjoy as a shot or sipping cocktail. This recipe is courtesy of Jim Beam.

INGREDIENTS

 1 oz. bourbon

 1 oz. lemon sour

 GLASSWARE
Coupe or shot glass

1   Place all of the ingredients in a cocktail shaker, fill it two-thirds of the way with ice, and shake until chilled.

2   Strain over ice into a chilled coupe or shot glass and enjoy.

EXTRA EASY AND SUPER SIMPLE

No concept is more sacred to the Home Bartender series than the idea that making tasty cocktails should be a breeze. And nowhere is that embraced more than in this chapter, where only the very simplest and easiest concoctions have earned their place. But just because most of these recipes have only two or three ingredients, that doesn't mean they don't still pack a punch of flavor! From the Rusty Nail to the Fire Extinguisher to the Gold Furnace, these drinks save you the time and effort of putting together a complicated cocktail so you can spend more time enjoying it.

JACK & GINGER

Courtesy of Jack Daniel's, this cocktail is sure to refresh and reinvigorate. The fresh, sweet, and slightly spicy flavor of ginger ale is always a great companion to Tennessee whiskey.

INGREDIENTS

 1 oz. Jack Daniel's Old No. 7 Tennessee whiskey

 3 oz. ginger ale

 1 lemon or lime wedge (garnish)

GLASSWARE
Collins glass

1 Fill a glass with ice and build the drink in it, adding the ingredients (except the garnish) in the order they are listed.

2 Gently stir until chilled and garnish with the wedge of lemon or lime.

SNAKE BITE

Between the sharpness of the tart lime juice and the hefty kick of Canadian whiskey, it's easy to see how this cocktail got its name.

INGREDIENTS

3 oz. Canadian whiskey

¾ oz. lime juice

GLASSWARE
Shot glass

1   Place all of the ingredients in a cocktail shaker, fill it two-thirds of the way with ice, and shake until chilled.

2   Strain into a glass and enjoy.

RUSTY NAIL

A perfect pairing of Scotch whisky and the very whisky it's made from. We like to add a little more Scotch than Drambuie, but feel free to experiment with the ratio.

INGREDIENTS

 2 oz. Scotch whisky

 ⅔ oz. Drambuie

 GLASSWARE
Rocks glass

1 Place all of the ingredients in a cocktail shaker, fill it two-thirds of the way with ice, and shake until chilled.

2 Strain into a glass, and enjoy.

GODFATHER

Named for the 1970s classic, this drink is said to have been a favorite of Marlon Brando's.

INGREDIENTS

2 oz. Scotch whisky

1 oz. amaretto

GLASSWARE

Rocks glass

1 Place all of the ingredients in a cocktail shaker, fill it two-thirds of the way with ice, and shake until chilled.

2 Strain over ice into a glass and enjoy.

GOLDDIGGER

Spicy and aromatic, whiskey and cinnamon schnapps make a perfect pair.

INGREDIENTS

1 oz. whiskey

1 oz. Goldschläger

GLASSWARE

Rocks glass

1 Place all of the ingredients in a cocktail shaker, fill it two-thirds of the way with ice, and shake until chilled.

2 Strain into a glass and enjoy.

BUFFALO BOWTIE

A simple but delicious twist on a Highball! We recommend using Buffalo Trace.

INGREDIENTS

 1½ oz. bourbon

 I oz. peach syrup

 Ginger ale

 Lime "bow tie" (garnish)

GLASSWARE

 Collins glass

1   Combine the bourbon and the peach syrup over ice in a highball glass.

2   Fill the glass with ginger ale and garnish the drink with a lime bow tie.

JAVA JACK SHOT

This sweet, strong concoction is great as either a shot or sipper.

INGREDIENTS

 1 oz. Jack Daniel's Old No. 7 Tennessee whiskey

 1 oz. coffee liqueur

GLASSWARE
Shot glass or cocktail glass

1 Combine ingredients and serve the drink in a chilled shot or cocktail glass.

HONEYCHATA

Full of sugar and spice, this sweet, smooth blend of rum, bourbon, cinnamon, and honey is a great after-dinner sipper.

INGREDIENTS

 1 oz. honey whiskey

 1 oz. RumChata

 GLASSWARE
Rocks or shot glass

1 Place all of the ingredients in a cocktail shaker, fill it two-thirds of the way with ice, and shake until chilled.

2 Strain over ice into a chilled rocks or shot glass and enjoy.

FIRE EXTINGUISHER

Sipped side by side, apple cider and Jack Daniel's fiery cinnamon liqueur make a perfect pair.

INGREDIENTS

 1 oz. cinnamon whiskey

 1 pint hard apple cider

GLASSWARE
 Rocks glass

1 Combine and pour into a chilled glass.

GOLD FURNACE

If you're looking to light a fire in your belly, this sweet and savory triple-spiced concoction will do the trick.

INGREDIENTS

1 oz. cinnamon whiskey

1 oz. Goldschläger

Tabasco, to taste

GLASSWARE

Shot glass

1 Place all of the ingredients, except for the Tabasco, in a cocktail shaker, fill it two-thirds of the way with ice, and shake until chilled.

2 Strain into a glass, add Tabasco to taste, and enjoy.

MAKER'S MULE

A sweet, full-bodied bourbon like Maker's Mark is the ultimate foil for chilled yet fiery ginger beer.

 1½ oz. bourbon

 1 splash lime juice

 Cold ginger beer

 1 lime slice (garnish)

 1 mint sprig (garnish)

 GLASSWARE
Copper mug

1 In a copper mug, add ice. Pour in the bourbon, add a splash of lime juice, and fill to top with ginger beer.

2 Garnish with a lime slice and mint sprig.

BOURBON SWEET TEA

Bourbon is a favorite drink of the South, and so is sweet tea. What could be more natural than adding them together to create a refreshing and delicious beverage perfect for beating the heat?

INGREDIENTS

Juice of ½ lemon

1 oz. bourbon

4 oz. sweet tea

4 lemon slices (garnish)

GLASSWARE

Pint glass

1 Squeeze the juice from ½ lemon into a pitcher.

2 Add ice, then pour in the bourbon and sweet tea. Stir until thoroughly mixed.

3 Pour into individual glasses and garnish each with a lemon slice. Enjoy!

FAMILY MEAL

This cocktail is the ultimate afternoon pick-me-up, with cold brew concentrate adding a real kick of flavor and caffeine. Although it can be made with any cola, we love Mexican Coke (it's made with real cane sugar). We also recommend using Maker's Mark bourbon.

INGREDIENTS

¼ oz. cold brew coffee concentrate

1½ oz. bourbon

Mexican Coke, as needed

1 lemon peel (garnish)

GLASSWARE

Sour glass

1 Fill a glass with ice and add the coffee and bourbon.

2 Gently stir until chilled. Top with Mexican Coke and finish with oil from a strip of lemon peel.

BLACK DOG

This Manhattan-adjacent cocktail swaps out bitters for blackberry brandy.

INGREDIENTS

 1 ½ oz. bourbon

 ½ oz. sweet vermouth

 ½ oz. blackberry brandy

GLASSWARE

 Rocks glass

1 Place all of the ingredients in a cocktail shaker, fill it two-thirds of the way with ice, and shake until chilled.

2 Strain into a glass and enjoy.

FOUR ROSES SKYSCRAPER

According to cocktail lore, the Skyscraper was invented by an artist who loved Manhattans. Wanting something a little lighter to drink during the day, she turned it into a tall drink by topping it off with ginger ale. This 1959 recipe from Four Roses keeps things from getting too sugary by using soda water instead.

INGREDIENTS

2 oz. bourbon

2/3 oz. sweet vermouth

Soda water

GLASSWARE

Sour glass

1 Fill the shaker with cracked ice, and jigger in Four Roses and sweet vermouth, three parts to one.

2 Stir until cold, pour into an ice-filled glass, and add soda. Enjoy!

BLACK MANHATTAN

The addition of black walnut bitters adds a smoky twist to this bourbon Manhattan.

INGREDIENTS

1½ oz. bourbon

1 oz. sweet vermouth (Carpano Antica Formula recommended)

2 to 3 dashes black walnut bitters

1 maraschino cherry (garnish)

GLASSWARE

Coupe or martini glass

1 Add bourbon, vermouth, bitters, and ice to mixing glass, stir until glass is frosted.

2 Strain into a chilled coupe or martini glass.

3 Add cherry. Stir.

SPRING MANHATTAN

This springtime spin on a Manhattan lightens things up a little with the addition of aperitif wine.

INGREDIENTS

2 oz. bourbon

1/2 oz. aperitif wine

1/2 oz. sweet vermouth

GLASSWARE
Cocktail glass or snifter

1   Stir all ingredients with ice in a mixing glass. Strain into a chilled cocktail glass.

MAKER'S MARK MANHATTAN

A slight variation on the classic Manhattan, with the bold, complex flavor of Maker's Mark 46, aged in seared French oak staves.

INGREDIENTS

 2 oz. Maker's Mark 46 bourbon whiskey

 ½ oz. sweet vermouth

 1 to 2 dashes Angostura bitters

 Brandy-soaked cherries (garnish)

GLASSWARE
Cocktail glass (chilled)

1 Pour the ingredients except for the garnish, into a mixing glass with ice cubes. Stir well.

2 Strain into a chilled cocktail glass.

3 Garnish with cherries.

FASHIONABLY OLD

Corsair's Grainiac incorporates oat, buckwheat, triticale, spelt, and quinoa into the standard bourbon mash bill. A surprising and complex bourbon, it makes for a nutty, earthy take on the Old Fashioned.

 2 oz. Corsair Grainiac 9 Grain Bourbon

 ¼ oz. demerara sugar

 3 dashes barrel-aged bitters

 Lemon peel (garnish)

GLASSWARE
Rocks glass

1 Combine all ingredients in a mixing glass with cracked ice. Stir for 30–45 seconds.

2 Strain into a rocks glass with fresh ice.

3 Garnish with the lemon peel..

FRISCO

A simple and oft-overlooked cocktail that predates Prohibition, the Frisco mellows the bite of rye whiskey with aromatic and slightly syrupy Bénédictine.

INGREDIENTS

 2 oz. rye whiskey

 1 oz. lemon juice

 1 splash Bénédictine

GLASSWARE

 Rocks glass

1 Place all of the ingredients in a cocktail shaker, fill it two-thirds of the way with ice, and shake until chilled.

2 Strain over ice into a glass and enjoy.

VANILLA SMASH

Warm vanilla, cool mint, and a generous helping of lemon make this summertime cocktail a smash hit.

INGREDIENTS

2 lemon wedges

6 to 8 mint leaves

1 oz. Jim Beam Vanilla bourbon whiskey

GLASSWARE

Rocks glass

1 Muddle the mint and lemon in a double rocks glass.

2 Fill with ice and add Jim Beam Vanilla.

HONEY AND LEMONADE

Crisp, tangy lemonade partners perfectly with Jim Beam Honey whiskey.

INGREDIENTS

 1½ oz. Jim Beam Honey whiskey

 6 to 8 oz. lemonade

 1 mint sprig (garnish)

GLASSWARE

 Mason jar

1 Fill a glass with ice and build the drink in it, adding the ingredients, except for the garnish, in the order they are listed.

2 Gently stir until chilled and garnish with the mint sprig.

HONEY AND TEA

The ultimate Southern duo: sweet tea and Jack Daniel's. This cocktail, courtesy of Jack Daniel's, is simple enough to throw together at the end of a long day and delicious enough to serve as a big batch party cocktail.

INGREDIENTS

 1½ oz. Jack Daniel's Tennessee Honey whiskey

 6 to 8 oz. tea

 1 mint sprig (garnish)

 GLASSWARE
Mason jar

1   Fill a glass with ice and build the drink in it, adding the ingredients, except for the garnish, in the order they are listed.

2   Gently stir until chilled and garnish with the mint.

SIGNATURE SERVE

Jim Beam Vanilla enhances the classic bourbon and cola cocktail.

INGREDIENTS

 1 oz. Jim Beam Vanilla bourbon whiskey

 2 oz. cola

 1 maraschino cherry (garnish)

GLASSWARE
Rocks glass

1 Fill a glass with ice and build the drink in it, adding the ingredients, except for the garnish, in the order they are listed.

2 Gently stir until chilled and garnish with the cherry.

QUARTER TANK OF GASOLINE

You might think you're unfamiliar with the flavor of sassafras, but if you've ever had root beer, you know what to expect. Here it lends that recognizable vanilla and anise-tinged wintergreen quality to this innovative take on the Whiskey Smash.

INGREDIENTS

 2 oz. Nelson's Green Brier Tennessee whiskey

 1 oz. sassafras syrup (see recipe to the right)

 ½ oz. lemon juice

 1 mint sprig (garnish)

GLASSWARE
 Rocks glass

1 Place all of the ingredients, except for the garnish, in a cocktail shaker, fill it two-thirds of the way with ice, and shake until chilled.

2 Strain the cocktail over ice into the rocks glass, garnish with fresh mint, and enjoy.

SASSAFRAS SYRUP

Place 3 sprigs of fresh mint, the zest of 2 lemons, and 1½ cups simple syrup (see page 7) in a large Mason jar and muddle. Add 1½ cups sassafras tea concentrate, shake to combine, and chill the syrup in the refrigerator overnight before using.

PANTHEON

Scotch whisky is the primary ingredient here, but creator Daisuke Ito sees it as Bénédictine modified with Scotch and lemon juice. That's fair—Bénédictine has a unique, honey-like flavor that is sweet without becoming medicinal like other similar liqueurs.

INGREDIENTS

 1 oz. Scotch whisky

 ½ oz. Bénédictine

 ½ oz. lemon juice

GLASSWARE

 Cocktail glass

1. Place all of the ingredients in a cocktail shaker, fill it two-thirds of the way with ice, and shake until chilled.

2. Strain into the cocktail glass and enjoy.

WHISKEY LEMONADE

Whiskey Lemonade was originally a drink borne of desperation, which came in the form of a vending machine that had only pink lemonade left inside. It turns out that in the right proportions, sweet lemonade and earthy whiskey are a match made in heaven. It's not a drink you want to make particularly strong, but a little bit of whiskey can take what is usually a cloyingly sweet beverage and temper it just the right amount.

INGREDIENTS

 1 oz. whiskey

 4 oz. pink lemonade

 1 lemon slice (garnish)

 GLASSWARE
Highball glass

1 Add the whiskey and lemonade to a highball glass filled with ice. Stir until thoroughly mixed.

2 Garnish with a lemon slice.

THE JUICE IS LOOSE

The Juice Is Loose is similar to the Whiskey Punch cocktail (page 47) in that it incorporates fruit flavors into a whiskey cocktail—a combination that many will be surprised they've never considered after tasting. The slight tartness of the cranberry complements the earthy tones of the whiskey, while the maraschino cherry garnish adds a splash of brightness to the drink's rosy glow. Elegant and delicious, The Juice Is Loose balances flavor and beauty.

INGREDIENTS

 1 oz. rye whiskey

 1 oz. cranberry or grape juice

 1 dash bitters

 1 maraschino cherry (garnish)

GLASSWARE

 Coupe

1 Place all of the ingredients, except for the garnish, in a cocktail shaker, fill it two-thirds of the way with ice, and shake until chilled.

2 Strain into a glass, garnish with the maraschino cherry, and enjoy.

LIQUID PB&J

What could be more comforting than a peanut butter and jelly sandwich? Those simple flavors hearken back to childhood, or at least simpler times. Smoky whiskey and sweet raspberry liqueur combine to evoke the feel of a jam sandwich, while crumbled peanuts rimming the glass provide the salty, earthy component that brings it all home. It's easy to make, easier to drink, and it will leave you feeling like you just put on your favorite old hoodie.

INGREDIENTS

 Crushed peanuts, for the rim

 1 oz. whiskey

 1 oz. raspberry liqueur

GLASSWARE

 Rocks glass

1 Wet the rim of a rocks glass and rim with crushed peanuts.

2 Add ice, then pour in the whiskey and raspberry liqueur. Stir together gently.

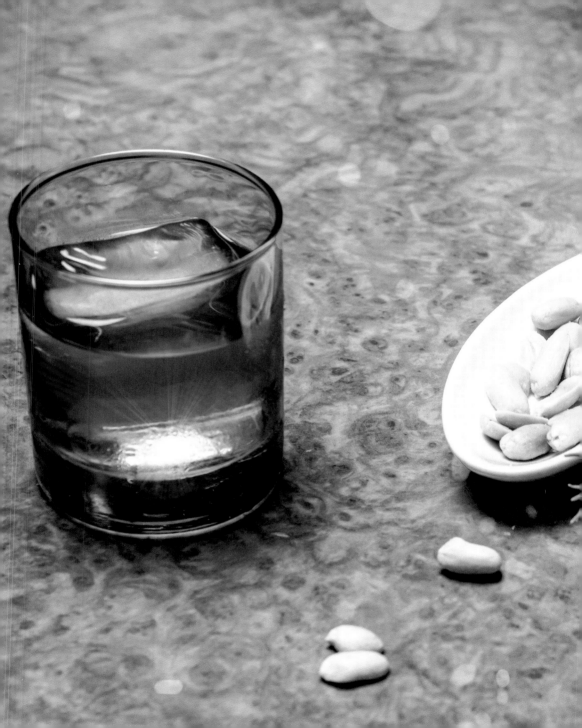

INDEX